ESSENTIAL MESSAGES FROM GOD'S SERVANTS

master*Work*®

Lessons from

SEVEN WORDS TO CHANGE YOUR FAMILY

by James MacDonald

MORAL EARTHQUAKES AND SECRET FAULTS

by O. S. Hawkins

WINTER 2007-08

LifeWay®
Biblical Solutions for Life®

Ross H. McLaren
Editor in Chief

Gena Rogers
Editor

Carolyn B. Gregory
Copy Editor

David Wilson
Graphic Designer

Melissa Finn
Lead Technical Specialist

David Apple
Adult Ministry Specialist

Send questions/comments to
  Editor, *MasterWork*
  One LifeWay Plaza
  Nashville, TN 37234-0175
  Or make comments on the Web at
  www.lifeway.com

Management Personnel

Bret Robbe, *Director*
Leadership and Adult Publishing
Ron Brown, Larry Dry, Ron Keck
Managing Directors
Leadership and Adult Publishing
David Francis, *Director*
Sunday School
Bill Craig, *Director*
Leadership and Adult Ministry
Gary Hauk, *Director Publishing*
LifeWay Church Resources

ACKNOWLEDGMENTS.–We believe the Bible has God for its author; salvation for its end; and truth, without any mixture of error, for its matter and that all Scripture is totally true and trustworthy. The 2000 statement of *The Baptist Faith and Message* is our doctrinal guideline.

Lessons by James MacDonald are condensed from *Seven Words to Change Your Family* (Chicago: Moody Press, 2002). Used by permission of Moody Press. All rights reserved.

Lessons by S. Hawkins are condensed from *Moral Earthquakes and Secret Faults* (Nashville: Broadman & Holman Publishers, 2006). Used by permission. All rights reserved.

Unless otherwise indicated, all Scripture quotations in the lessons from *Seven Words to Change Your Family*, and those marked NASB, are from the *New American Standard Bible*®, Copyright © 1960, 1962, 1963, 1968, 1971, 1972, 1975, 1977, 1995 by the Lockman Foundation. Used by permission. Scripture quotations marked NIV are from the Holy Bible, *New International Version*, copyright © 1973, 1978, 1984 by International Bible Society. Scripture quotations marked NKJV are from the *New King James Version*. Copyright © 1979, 1982, Thomas Nelson, Inc., Publishers. Scripture quotations marked KJV are from the *King James Version*.

Unless otherwise indicated, all Scripture quotations in the lessons from *Moral Earthquakes and Secret Faults* are from the *New King James Version*, copyright © 1979, 1980, 1982 by Thomas Nelson, Inc. Used by permission. Quotations in the "How to Become a Christian" article or those marked HCSB are taken from the *Holman Christian Standard Bible*®, copyright © 1999, 2000, 2001, 2002 by Holman Bible Publishers. Used by permission. This translation is available in a Holman Bible and can be ordered through LifeWay Christian Stores.

MasterWork: Essential Messages from God's Servants (ISSN 1542-703X) is published quarterly by LifeWay Christian Resources of the Southern Baptist Convention, One LifeWay Plaza, Nashville, Tennessee 37234; Thom Rainer, President. © Copyright 2007 LifeWay Christian Resources of the Southern Baptist Convention. All rights reserved. Single subscription to individual address, $26.35 per year. If you need help with an order, WRITE LifeWay Church Resources Customer Service, One LifeWay Plaza, Nashville, Tennessee 37234-0113; For subscriptions, FAX (615) 251-5818 or E-MAIL subscribe@lifeway.com. For bulk shipments mailed quarterly to one address, FAX (615) 251-5933 or E-MAIL CustomerService@lifeway.com. Order ONLINE at *www.lifeway.com*. Mail address changes to: *MasterWork*, One LifeWay Plaza, Nashville, TN 37234-0113.

Printed in the United States of America.

Cover photo credit:
© James Nazz/CORBIS

table of Contents

ABOUT THE WRITERS

James MacDonald

is the founding and senior pastor of Harvest Bible Chapel in the northwestern suburbs of Chicago. James's teaching can be heard on the daily, 30-minute radio program "Walk in the Word," which airs across North America.

James received his master's degree from Trinity Divinity School and his doctorate from Phoenix Seminary. He and his wife, Kathy, have three children and reside in Chicago.

AMY SUMMERS wrote the personal learning activities and teaching plans for these lessons. Amy is an experienced writer for LifeWay Bible study curriculum, a wife, a mother, and a Sunday School leader from Arden, North Carolina. She is a graduate of Baylor University and Southwestern Baptist Theological Seminary.

ABOUT THIS STUDY

Read the following verses from your Bible and complete the phrase for each.

2 Thessalonians 2:16
God's hope is _____

Hebrews 6:19
God's hope is _____

1 Peter 1:3
God's hope is _____

Pray that God will use this study to anchor you and your family in His good, eternal, and living hope.

Seven Words to Change Your Family

Hope is one of the greatest needs in the families of our day. Someone has said that if you have lost hope, you have lost everything, and far too many families I meet and talk with have lost their hope. They are not seeking transformation; they are seeking survival. They are not believing God for a better tomorrow at home; they just hope to have a home tomorrow.

Maybe at this moment you are very discouraged about the needs you see in your family. God loves you and is working today to bring lasting joy and transformation to your family. That's what He is doing every day in our world. God wants to do a miracle in your family, and He wants to begin that work today through you. Unless you have hope, unless you believe that God can and will bring transformation to your family, the rest of the study will be a waste of time.

Before we begin, I want to give an overview of what you'll be studying. The seven words consist of:

1. Three *healing* words to help you conquer the pain of the past and get on a new page for the wonderful future God has for you.
2. Three *building* words to help you put good habits in place of ones that may have been more negative.
3. One *transforming* word. There is something you must have every step of the way. You can turn to it right away if you want, but it fits far better at the end as a covering for all the wonderful things I am trusting God will do for you and your family.

What's in the coming pages can bring lasting change to the very circumstances you're facing. I pray that God will use this study to bring healing and health to the family needs that are on your heart.

James MacDonald

Forgiveness

day One

Jesus on Forgiveness

> "Whenever you stand praying, forgive, if you have anything against anyone, so that your Father who is in heaven will also forgive you your transgressions" (Mark 11:25).

Jesus didn't simply talk about forgiveness. He modeled it in His everyday life. From the woman caught in adultery (John 8:1-11) to His final words on the cross—"Father, forgive them; for they do not know what they are doing" (Luke 23:34)—Jesus was and is all about forgiveness.

How about you? If you profess to be a follower of Jesus Christ, are you all about forgiveness?
❏ **Not at all, and I don't want to be.**
❏ **Mostly, except for that one person.**
❏ **I wish I were; unforgiveness is eating me alive.**
❏ **Absolutely!**

> "Forgive, and you will be forgiven" (Luke 6:37, NKJV).

No doubt there are countless people who have injured you; they have said false things about you; they have wounded you with their actions and reactions. Regardless of where it came from, the fallout from unforgiveness is huge. And nowhere is this seen more clearly than in the home. So much of the anger and strife that exists in the family today is rooted in people's unwillingness to forgive.

It's important for us to be on the same page, so here's our working definition of forgiveness: *Forgiveness is a decision to release a person from the obligation that resulted when he or she injured you.*

I pray that as you study this material God will reveal whom you need to forgive, the specifics of that forgiveness, and that you will make a choice to forgive them.

Let's go to Matthew 18 and look at a story Jesus told about forgiveness. The context of the passage is conflict resolution. Jesus had been teaching, in effect, "If you have a problem with somebody, work it out. If you can, let it go. If you can't, sit down with him or her and work it out. If the person won't resolve the matter, take somebody along and try to work it out. If that bombs, take some elders from your church and make the matter right." Nothing makes the Lord happier than to see His children living in harmony, so Jesus did a lot of teaching on this subject.

"Peter came and said to Him, 'Lord, how often shall my brother sin against me and I forgive him? Up to seven times?' " (Matt. 18:21). Jesus responded, "I do not say to you, up to seven times, but up to seventy times seven" (v. 22). That's a lot of forgiveness! The point is, don't keep track. Forgiveness is not to be measured or counted but given freely.

To make His case, Jesus told a parable—a fictitious story that makes a point.

> "Forgiveness is not to be measured or counted but given freely."
> —James MacDonald

Read Matthew 18:23-30 in your Bible. Fill in the chart to contrast the two slaves.

	Slave 1	Slave 2
Who and what he owed		
Request he made		
Response of the person he owed		

Jesus' story contains several principles that should bring us to the decision of forgiveness. First, notice that the rationalizations used for not forgiving are foolish. Peter was looking for a way out of forgiveness. He was looking for an excuse. "Lord, what if I forgive someone seven times? Is that enough? Can I go this far and no further? Is there a person I don't have to forgive? Is there a sin I don't have to forgive? Is there a point at which I don't have to forgive anymore? This forgive-everyone-everything-all-the-time stuff is just way too much! I need to put some limits on this forgiveness thing."

Peter was looking for a rationalization. Jesus responded, "No, you are to forgive everyone, for everything, all the time—unilateral forgiveness! Don't look for a way out."

Rationalizations

Often this need to forgive is more apparent in others than in our own life and family, but when the problem is our own, we struggle to make it happen, choosing instead to offer foolish rationalizations that won't stand up before God. Here are five of the most common. Maybe you've used some of them yourself.

As you read the following rationalizations, star the ones you are using in your life right now. In the margin beside each rationalization you star, briefly describe the situation in which you are using that rationalization.

1. *"The hurt is too big."* Wouldn't you think that the bigger the hurt, the more you would want to get rid of it? It's not the little burden we need to off-load; it's the big one that's weighing us down and crushing our joy. The bigger the hurt, the more we need to forgive.

2. *"Time will heal it."* It might scar over, but you know it hasn't healed because when someone mentions the delicate subject or brings up the names of the people involved, the pain is still very real. You can come face-to-face with that person toward whom you harbor unforgiveness, or you can be standing in the shower when a certain event comes to mind—and you know time is not healing it because it's still as painful as before. Time heals nothing.

3. *"I'll forgive when they come and say they're sorry."* They're not coming. If you never forgive unless the people say they're sorry, you will hardly ever forgive. And if they should come to make an apology, your unforgiveness will prevent you from being ready to receive them.

4. *"I can't forgive if I can't forget."* You will never forget until you forgive. Forgiveness is both the crisis and the process of putting a person's sin behind you. It's a choice that begins the process of forgetting. Unforgiveness binds the offense to your heart and ensures you will never forget.

5. *"If I forgive, they'll just do it again."* Forgiveness does not mean you have to put yourself at risk. Unforgiveness is a burden. If there is a chance the person may wound you again, that is all the more reason to forgive. Otherwise you'll be carrying two burdens, either one of which is sufficient to destroy your life.

The fallout of not forgiving is huge. When you decide not to release a person but instead to nurse the injury and harbor the resentment, look out for some major consequences. You can see this so clearly in the life of the unmerciful servant.

Read the remainder of Jesus' parable in Matthew 18:31-35. List consequences the servant faced because of his unforgiving attitude.

_____

_____

Most people know that unforgiveness leads to relational fallout and bitterness, but it can also lead to stupidity. How crazy was the unmerciful servant to throw his pal in jail? That'll get the money back real soon! It doesn't make sense. Here's why. He didn't want the money back. He wanted revenge. That's what often fuels a heart of unforgiveness—a desire to see the other person suffer, to make him or her feel what you feel.

The unmerciful servant also lost the respect of his fellow servants. Scripture says they were "deeply grieved" at the way he was acting (v. 31). If you are harboring resentment and unforgiveness in your heart, I guarantee there are people who don't want to be around you anymore because you are always negative and focused on the pain.

Then there was the humiliation the servant experienced before the king. Check out what he said when he was called back before the king—nothing! The king said, "I forgave you all of this, and you can't forgive this little bit?" The servant was ashamed and embarrassed. He couldn't spout a syllable.

Who is the king in the story? God. Who is the servant in the story? Each of us. And we are headed for the very same appointment someday. If we harbor resentment and unforgiveness, God is going to say, "I forgave you everything, and you couldn't even do this?" The fallout is huge.

Lasting Consequences

"How good and pleasant it is when brothers live together in unity! ... It is as if the dew of Hermon were falling on Mount Zion. For there the Lord bestows his blessing, even life forevermore" (Ps. 133:1,3, NIV).

Read Psalm 133:1,3 in the margin. What are the results of choosing to forgive? _____

The act of forgiving affects both the body and the mind. Forgiving people are more stable. They have stronger relationships. People who forgive are often happier and less prone to depression and anxiety.

Scientific findings showing physical and emotional benefits to forgiveness should not surprise followers of Christ. We serve the King of kings and Lord of lords who made us. He knows how our bodies work.

Here's another lesson found in Jesus' story in Matthew 18: The consequences of not forgiving are lasting. Look again at verses 34 and 35. They are the most important in the parable. "His lord, moved with anger, handed him over to the torturers until he should repay all that was owed him." Unforgiveness is torturous. If you refuse to forgive those who injure you, life will become for you a massive torture chamber where nearly every human encounter passes through the grid of your own unresolved pain. If you continue living this way, you'll experience the exhaustion of hauling around all the things you've been unwilling to forgive.

The consequences of unforgiveness are experienced not only in this life, but also in the life to come. "My heavenly Father will also do the same to you, if each of you does not forgive his brother from your heart" (v. 35). This is not the only place Jesus discussed the eternal consequences of failing to forgive.

Read Matthew 6:14-15 in your Bible. Write the two if/then statements contained in that passage.

If _____, then _____.

But if _____, then _____.

God says, "You're going to be judged by the standard you used with others." The person who over a lifetime refuses to forgive ultimately reveals that he or she has never really comprehended or received the eternal forgiveness God offers in Jesus Christ. What cancer is to the body, unforgiveness is to the family. If you won't forgive, God won't bless or heal or restore or reach your loved ones.

Read James 2:13 in the margin.

What sobering truth did you discover?

"Judgment will be merciless to one who has shown no mercy; mercy triumphs over judgment" (Jas. 2:13).

_____

What encouraging truth did you discover?

_____

Pray, asking God for strength to obey Him and forgive those against whom you've been harboring bitterness.

Here are three things forgiveness is not:

1. *Forgiveness is not enabling.* Suppose you said to me, "My mother has an overspending problem, and she always borrows money from me. She wastes my cash on foolish impulse purchases." Forgiveness does not mean you have to drop by your mother's house with credit cards. "I'll show her how forgiving I am!" Forgiveness does not require you help the person do the thing for which you have forgiven them. That is enabling.

2. *Forgiveness is not rescuing.* Imagine that my 16-year-old son decides to take our family car out for a joyride. He steals the keys, takes off, and ends up driving the car up a tree. As a parent, I have a choice. Forgiveness does not mean rescuing my son from the consequences of bad behavior. I don't have to try to bribe the judge or otherwise eliminate the repercussions that God may use to teach my son some important lessons.

3. *Forgiveness is not risking.* Let's pretend that my father becomes angry and violent when he drinks. Every time he does, he really hurts me. I must forgive him, but that doesn't mean I have to accept his invitation to the New Year's Eve bash. Forgiveness does not require putting myself in harm's way.

How Do Families Forgive?

Forgiveness comes in two parts. It begins with a decision, an act of my will. We call this the crisis of forgiveness. When I make the choice to release a person from the obligation that resulted when he or she injured me, I am completing the crisis of forgiveness. I am not looking for vengeance; I am not trying to get even; I am not wishing for bad things to happen to them; and I am not focused on their failure. I am not thinking about them at all. I am releasing them from all obligation that resulted when they hurt me.

"Forgive us our debts, as we also have forgiven our debtors" (Matt. 6:12).

When you have forgiven someone, what debt does he or she owe you?
❑ **An apology**   ❑ **A promise never to do it again**
❑ **Nothing**
❑ **He/she needs to be miserable for a while**

Maybe you remember completing the crisis of forgiveness in the past, only to retract that act of grace and begin again to nurse and nurture the injury of someone else's sin. Maybe you have responded publicly in a church service and committed yourself to forgiveness or knelt alone and promised God you would forgive but fell into your old patterns of hate or resentment when you crossed paths with the one you had chosen to forgive. If that is your experience, you need to understand the difference between the crisis and the process of forgiveness. Beyond the crisis is the process of forgiveness, without which you will never experience the healing that forgiveness can bring. In the crisis of forgiveness we say, "I choose to forgive," but in the process we say, "I will treat you as though it never happened." Here is how that process works:

Crisis of Forgiveness:
"I choose to forgive."

Process of Forgiveness:
"I will treat you as though it never happened."

1. I won't bring the offense up to the person, except for his or her benefit.
2. I won't bring the offense up to others.
3. I won't bring the offense up to myself. I will not go over it and think about it and dwell upon it.

Read 2 Corinthians 10:5 and Philippians 4:8 in your Bible. How can living out these verses help you when those offenses crop back up in your mind?

_____

_____

When you are doing the three steps above effectively, you are succeeding in the process of forgiveness. This is a lesson I am learning little by little in my own life. I could share several acts of forgiveness I have been working on for 10 or 15 years. I am still in the process. Here is the key: When I fail in the process, I have to go back to the crisis. If you do that faithfully, you will get free.

One day I was driving along with my oldest son, Luke, and we passed by a restaurant. He asked, "Dad, how come we don't eat there anymore?" I could hardly believe what came out of my mouth: "Because I used to eat lunch there a lot with somebody who really hurt me! I don't like the person anymore, so I don't like the restaurant anymore."

That comment was a failure in the process of forgiveness. I brought up a matter about which I had not really forgiven someone and not only reviewed it myself but communicated it to someone else. In that instance I was the one who was sinning. To make that right I needed to return to the crisis of forgiveness and say, "Lord, forgive me for dwelling on the failure of that person. I have forgiven that person, Lord. Forgive me for my sin. You have forgiven me so much. How can I fail to forgive others?" I had to return to the crisis and then begin afresh to live in the process of forgiveness. In time I will begin to experience the incredible healing and blessing that God grants to the life of the truly forgiving person.

Have you failed somewhere in the process of forgiveness? Write the person's name in the blank below and then read the prayer out loud as your commitment.

_Lord, forgive me for dwelling on the failure of _____.
I have forgiven him/her, Lord. Forgive me for my sin. You have forgiven me so much. How can I fail to forgive?_

When Will I See the Blessing?

Because our hearts often mislead us, people will sometimes ask me, "How can I know if I have truly forgiven someone?" To answer that question, let's look at Ephesians 4:31-32, where the apostle Paul writes, "Let all bitterness and wrath and anger and clamor and slander be put away from you, along with all malice. Be kind to one another, tender-hearted, forgiving each other, just as God in Christ also has forgiven you." In these important verses we see both the fallout of unforgiveness and the blessings of true forgiveness.

When you forgive, damaging emotions are eliminated. There are six damaging emotions listed in Ephesians 4:31. Let's go over each one.

1. *Bitterness.* The Greek word translated as *bitterness* carries the idea of cutting, and cut it does. Bitterness cuts our insides to ribbons. It is the fretting, irritable state of mind, the perpetual animosity that inclines a person to a harsh opinion of others. Bitterness is the sour, crabby demeanor. It's acid on the heart; it's a scowl on the face; it's venom in the words. So many people are bitter because they have failed at the point of forgiveness.

Read Hebrews 12:15. What will happen if you don't allow God to deal with the bitterness in your life?

2. *Wrath.* This is a deeply settled indignation that flows from constant unresolved issues. Wrath makes the heart like a furnace. The more you stoke it, the hotter it gets—but always simmering, always burning just beneath the surface.

3. *Anger.* Anger is a temporary excitement, an outburst of rage. It's the fist through the wall, the broken glass. It explodes and dissipates. Anger frequently shows up in partnership with ...

4. *Clamor.* Clamor is the noise of relational strife. It's the loud self-assurance of the unforgiving person who requires everyone to hear his or her grievance.

Clamor is hold-still-you're-going-to-hear-me-on-this-whether-you-want-to-hear-it-or-not. It's a damaging emotion, a symptom of unforgiveness.

5. *Slander*. Slander is the depth of evil speech. It comes from the Greek word often translated "to blaspheme." Slanderous words are calculated words intended to injure. Slander is ready-aim-fire, I'm-going-to-say-this-and-I-don't-care-who-it-hurts. It's because of unforgiveness in the heart.

6. *Malice*. Malice is the evil inclination of the mind, the capacity to locate wrongdoing and do it. It means literally "bad-heartedness." Malice says, "I am going to feel this. I am not going to let go of this. I don't care what you say. I have every right to feel this way!"

Be brutally honest with yourself. Go back and write your initials next to each damaging emotion that is present in your life.

If any of these emotions are present in your life, you are destroying yourself. You're ripping a swath of destruction like a tornado across a Kansas wheat field. Worse, you are doing it to the people who love you, those closest to you. But when you choose to live by forgiveness, damaging emotions are gradually eliminated from your life.

Second, when you forgive, healing efforts are renewed. Verse 32 starts off by saying, "Be kind to one another." The word translated "be kind" is not a general comment about how you should treat your favorite people; it doesn't mean, "Be nice to the people you like." In the context it means, "Be kind—without reservation—to the very people you had to forgive." It's a fruit of forgiveness, and it's an action that reveals a heart change. Kindness when forced from an unforgiving heart only produces more anger. Have you ever been unforgiving toward your boss, and he didn't even know it? Then he comes by and asks, "Would you mind helping me with a few of these things? I am so swamped!" You're like, "I cannot believe he is asking me that again today!" You probably won't tell him, but your attitude reveals something is not right in your heart. You can't freely show kindness to that person. Where the capacity to show kindness is lacking, you know for sure that unforgiveness is lurking somewhere in the shadows.

Third, when you forgive, healing attitudes are restored. Tenderheartedness is a willingness to feel the pain of another. When you are ready to empathize, you'll begin to think, *As awful as the sin was, they must have been hurting*

When we forgive:

1. damaged emotions are eliminated
2. healing efforts are renewed
3. healing attitudes are restored
4. Christ's example is elevated

badly to have done that to me. When you begin to open your heart up to the pain of the other person, when you have a growing capacity to be tender-hearted toward the one who injured you, forgiveness is well under way.

Finally, when you forgive, Christ's example is elevated. "Be kind to one another, tender-hearted, forgiving each other, just as God in Christ also has forgiven you."

"Bear with each other and forgive whatever grievances you may have against one another. Forgive as the Lord forgave you" (Col. 3:13, NIV).

As you read Colossians 3:13 in the margin, underline the principle that is also taught in Ephesians 4:32.

How has Christ forgiven you? _____

How are you to forgive others? _____

Just like Christ forgave you. That's how we forgive. Just as fast. Just as freely. Just as fully. Just like Jesus. That's the way we are commanded to forgive.

The bottom line is: There are no enduring relationships without forgiveness. I'm sure you have a lot of dreams for your family. You will never see those dreams realized without forgiveness. If you want to make it to your golden wedding anniversary, it's going to require several major forgivenesses and a truckload of minor ones. If you can't deal in the forgiveness environment, then you will have a lot of pain in your family's future. But here's the good news: You can forgive. And God wants to help you. Never are we more like Christ than when we choose to forgive.

"Never are we more like Christ than when we choose to forgive."
—James MacDonald

Whose face have you been seeing throughout this study on forgiveness? Indicate your commitment to forgive this person by writing his or her name in the blank below (it may be the same or a different person than you recorded in Day 4).

I choose to forgive _____ **and release**

_____ **from his/her obligation to me.**

_____ **owes me nothing.**

To the Leader:

Each week you will be given two ideas for beginning the session. The first option will be a question or two to help you get the discussion rolling. The second option will require a little more interaction or activity from participants. Allow these suggestions to spark your own creativity so you can begin each session in a way that motivates your class to discuss and learn each week's material.

Before the Session

1. Write each of the seven words to change your family on placards and display each word the week it is studied. By the end of your study you will have seven powerful words displayed that will remind participants to be integrating those principles into their lives.
2. Prepare a large writing surface (board, poster, etc.) for use during the session.

During the Session

1. Ask: *What do you think are the most powerful words in the English language?* Write responses on the board, being sure to include *hope*. Discuss why each word is so powerful. OR Organize participants into groups and instruct them to list what they feel are the three greatest needs in families today. (Single adults can focus their answers on what singles need in their own one-person and extended families.) Allow groups to share their responses and explain why they chose them. FOR EITHER OPTION Ask why participants think Dr. MacDonald said hope is one of the greatest needs in families. Discuss the introductory overview on page 5. Explain: *Godly hope believes God can heal, build, and transform your family. In the next seven weeks we are going to explore seven powerful words that, if implemented, will meet every need and change every person and family represented in our class.*

2. Request that participants identify negative cycles that destroy families. Ask what must occur if those negative cycles are to be broken. [If they're having trouble, ask someone to read the title of Week 1.] Ask someone to read Dr. MacDonald's definition of forgiveness from Day 1 (p. 6). Share that Jesus told a parable to illustrate how forgiveness releases a person from a debt. Discuss the second activity of Day 1 (p. 7). Inquire: *Do we more often see the king's actions and attitudes or the slave's actions and attitudes toward forgiveness in our world (and ourselves)?* Ask participants to listen as you read Matthew 18:21-22 and determine whether they think Peter's attitude toward forgiveness more closely resembled

the king or the slave. Explain that Peter, like most people, was looking for a way out of forgiveness.

3. Request that participants share from Day 2 the five rationalizations for unforgiveness. Ask why Jesus insists we throw away our excuses and forgive everyone for everything every time. Explain that the fallout of not forgiving is huge. Use the second activity in Day 2 (p. 9) and Dr. MacDonald's comments in Days 2 and 3 to discuss consequences of unforgiveness.

4. Discuss the second activity of Day 3 (p. 10). Explain that God cannot pour forgiveness into a heart that is shut up tight with unforgiveness against someone else. Ask: *Does forgiving have as many lasting consequences as not forgiving? Explain.* Go back and discuss the first activity of Day 3. Allow volunteers to share how they have experienced blessing and real life as a result of forgiving someone.

5. Explain that we must learn how to truly forgive if we want to experience God's blessings. Request that participants share from Day 4 the two parts necessary for forgiveness [crisis and process]. Allow volunteers to share which of the three steps in the process of forgiveness is most difficult for them and why. Discuss the second activity of Day 4 (p. 13). Ask: *What are we to do if we fail in the process of forgiveness?* Invite someone to read aloud James 2:13 (p. 11). Ask how that verse challenges and encourages them through this whole forgiveness process.

6. Request that someone read Ephesians 4:31-32. Ask how we can know if we have truly forgiven someone. Ask the class to follow along in their Bibles as you read aloud Genesis 4:1-8. Ask which of the six damaging emotions discussed in Day 5 are evident in Cain's life and who was destroyed because of his unforgiveness. Ask: *Do you think a failure to forgive someone outside your family can have a negative impact inside your home? Explain.* Share that to renew hope and joy in our families, we must forgive everyone. Inquire: *Do you think kindness and tenderheartedness only come after forgiveness, or can they help you in the forgiving process? Explain.*

7. Ask volunteers to read Ephesians 4:32 and Colossians 3:13. Discuss the questions from Day 5 related to those verses (p. 16). Request that participants prayerfully consider the final activity in Day 5. Read Matthew 18:15,19-20. Urge participants to agree together that you all desire forgiveness and unity in your families. Allow volunteers to pray; then close the group in prayer.

Blessing

day One

What Is the Blessing?[1]

Deep within the heart of every person is a longing for parental approval. We search for it our whole lives. If we don't receive it from our parents, we search for it elsewhere, and our hearts are restless until the blessing is found. When we do receive the blessing, our lives take on a level of fulfillment and security that cannot be realized any other way.

Blessing is not some new psychological construct. It's been around for a long time. In fact, it shows up in the very first book of the Bible. Abraham had one miraculous son named Isaac; later Isaac had two sons, Jacob and Esau. Esau was born first and, according to the customs of the day, the substantive portion of the family wealth belonged to him; this was called the birthright. However, Isaac's wife, Rebecca, had a different plan in mind. She favored the younger son, Jacob, and so she and the "baby" conceived a plan to trick Isaac into giving his blessing not to the firstborn Esau but to him.

Read what happened next in Genesis 27:30-38 in your Bible. What did Esau do when he could not receive his father's blessing? (Concentrate on verses 34 and 38.)

Keep in mind that Esau was not some soft, effeminate, emotionally fragile man. He was a fisherman, a hunter, and a gamesman. And yet, as a grown adult, he wept like a baby because his father did not give the blessing to him. We can learn a lot from that.

Each of us is far more like Esau than we might want to admit. Deep within the heart of every person is a longing for parental approval. We want to feel confident that our mother and father know us, love us, and value us, that they are proud of us and recognize our accomplishments. Parental blessing is a universal longing.

I've heard some people say, "I don't need the blessing; my parents didn't give it, and I wouldn't receive it if they did." Yet I've watched those same people be absolutely transformed when they did receive the blessing. Almost instantly they moved from a place of insecurity to one of confidence. I've heard someone say, "I wouldn't let my old man give me a nickel. In fact, I can hardly stand to look at him!" And yet I've watched that same individual get on a plane and rush across the country to plead for a word of love and commendation at his father's deathbed. There is something within the heart of every person that longs for the blessing. Our Father in heaven made us that way.

Read Matthew 3:17 in the margin. When we follow God's example, what are we essentially declaring when we bless our children?

_____

You may be saying to yourself, "I already know I didn't get this from my parents." Maybe that's true. But if life in Christ is about anything, it's about breaking the chains of the past. Perhaps you're the first-generation Christian who can draw a line in the sand and declare, "The blessing is going to start with me." What an opportunity God has given you! You can break the chains of the past! You can be the first who will do the things that God in His Word has commanded be done.

Perhaps you don't have kids of your own. But how many children are in your life? How many children are sitting at your feet whose parents don't have the wisdom to make sure their children get this blessing? Every adult has some access to children and can meet this God-given need.

Record the names of children to whom you can give a

blessing. _____

_____

"There is something within the heart of every person that longs for the blessing. Our Father in heaven made us that way."
—James MacDonald

"Behold, a voice out of the heavens said, 'This is My beloved Son, in whom I am well-pleased' " (Matt. 3:17).

day Two

How Can We Communicate the Blessing?

There's a five-step process by which every parent can make sure the blessing is regularly and powerfully communicated to his or her children. We'll talk about the first step today.

1. MEANINGFUL TOUCH

Read Genesis 27:26-27. How was the blessing conveyed to Jacob? Underline your answer.

A handshake   A written contract   A kiss

Jacob is 40 years old or more, and his daddy is kissing him. I love it! When it comes to demonstrating affection physically, most of us are severely constipated. It's kind of tragic when a boy just 13 or 14 years old is uncomfortable expressing affection to his father. Or maybe the father is so stiff that he can't even express affection when the children are small.

Much has been written about the healing, nurturing, and affirming power of touch, and it's so sad when this is neglected in the home. Meaningful touch can lower blood pressure, protect our children from seeking sexual intimacy prior to marriage, and add up to two years to one's life.

We offer lame reasons for not touching our children in meaningful ways. You've heard them, haven't you?

"I show my love by my actions." As if communicating love and blessing to our children is a show. A kid should not have to connect the dots to get a message of love and affection from his or her parents. Our child's life is to be immersed in love, acceptance, and blessing.

Read the passage from Mark printed in the margin. How did Jesus demonstrate love and blessing to children?

_____

"They were bringing children to Him so that He might touch them; but the disciples rebuked them. But when Jesus saw this, He was indignant and said to them, 'Permit the children to come to Me; do not hinder them' … And He took them in His arms and began blessing them, laying His hands on them" (Mark 10:13-14,16).

"It makes me feel uncomfortable." If touching your children in ways that make them feel loved and affirmed is hard for you, it's probably because you did not receive such physical affection from your parents. May God help us to break those patterns of neglect and be everything He has called us to be for the children in our lives.

"It's not that important. I can make it up to them in other ways." When I hear parents make this excuse, I start to get mad. I'm not asking you to cut off your right arm here; just use your arms and your eyes and your lips to send—without words—a life-changing message to your kids. I can't emphasize too much how very important this is.

"I don't want to go overboard." I can't tell you how many times I've heard, "I am so messed up! I just can't deal with life because Mom and Dad used to hug and kiss me so often they just made me crazy!" As if!

On the line below, draw a star to indicate the amount of blessing you have received through meaningful touch. Make a check mark to indicate how much blessing you bestow through touch.

_____

No blessing   **Overflowing blessing**

Tomorrow we'll talk about the next step in communicating the blessing.

day Three

How Can We Communicate the Blessing? (Part 2)

2. SPOKEN WORDS

A blessing is not a blessing until it is spoken. The most powerful way to build upon the foundation of meaningful touch is through the words you say to your children.

Read the verses printed in the margin and complete this statement:

Spoken words have the negative power to _____

_____

and the positive power to _____

_____ .

"The tongue has the power of life and death" (Prov. 18:21, NIV).

"Reckless words pierce like a sword, but the tongue of the wise brings healing" (Prov. 12:18, NIV).

"The tongue that brings healing is a tree of life, but a deceitful tongue crushes the spirit" (Prov. 15:4, NIV).

In our homes and with our children, the tongue has the power to destroy, but it also has the power to enrich and edify. Our words can build up and bless those we love. Here are kinds of words that should ring out relentlessly in the hallways of our homes:

1. *Words of affection.* Over and over and over in our homes, the words "I love you" should be spoken. From husband to wife, from wife to husband, from children to parents, from parents to children. "I love you" should be the constant refrain in the beautiful music families make together.

2. *Words of reconciliation.* We are all fallen people, not just in principle but also in practice. James 3:2 reminds us that "we all stumble in many ways." Those who live most closely with you know your flaws best. Yet

when was the last time you said to the people in your family, "I'm sorry. I was wrong. Please forgive me"?

3. *Words of vision.* When we speak words of vision over our children, we paint a picture of effectiveness regarding their lives. "You're going to do something great with your life." "You're going to make a difference in this world." Words of vision build hope and confidence.

4. *Words of security.* We need to say little things that imprint upon our children's hearts a sense of who God has created them to be.

Read Ephesians 4:29. What should result from the words we speak to children (and others)?

_____

The problem in our day is that spoken words take time. Mom tries to rush a few words in the bridal room while the photographer is there—but it's too late. All those things she wanted to say to her precious daughter, but now the years are gone, and with them the opportunity to communicate the blessing. Dad tries to slip a few words in just before his son jumps in the car and leaves for college. He can't believe the days have slipped away, and he aches about all the things he wanted to communicate—but never did.

God forgive us for our silence when our words could make such a difference. Proverbs 3:27 says, "Do not withhold good from those to whom it is due, when it is in your power to do it." That's the blessing.

Whom do you need to bless with spoken words

today?_____

Briefly record the words of blessing you will speak to

this person(s). _____

_____

Tomorrow we'll talk about the next three steps in communicating the blessing.

"The tongue is a small part of the body, and yet it boasts of great things" (Jas. 3:5).

How Can We Communicate the Blessing? (Part 3)

3. AFFIRMING YOUR CHILD'S VALUE

Let's go back to Isaac's blessing of Jacob in Genesis 27:27. What did Isaac do after he kissed his son?

_____

At the heart of the parental blessing is a word picture that communicates, "You matter to us." "We care about you." "You are special and unique." Affirming value is critical to a developing child's identity.

It's hard to believe that Isaac actually smelled his 40-year old son, but that's what God's Word says. "The smell of my son is like the smell of a field which the Lord has blessed." It's a picture. It's as if Isaac is saying, "Do you know what I think of, Son, when I think of you? I see this field with grain growing. I hear the birds singing. I see the sun shining. And you're in the middle of the field, tall and strong." Special words are a powerful way to communicate love and affirmation and blessing to our children.

I read of some parents who, every Christmas Eve after their children were in bed, would put additional presents under the tree—one for each of their children. Written on each present was, "To Mom and Dad, From Jesus." On Christmas morning the parents would go through a little ritual: "Oh, what's this? Wow, look! You kids aren't the only ones who are getting presents today. We got some too, and they're from Jesus! You open them. We're just too excited to look. What do you think Jesus gave us?" Each child would open up the gift and inside they would discover a picture of themselves.

The parents would say, "That's what we get again this year. God gave us you!" What an incredible picture of blessing to communicate to your children! Isn't that fantastic?

4. SPIRITUAL VISION

Notice what Isaac said to Jacob in Genesis 27:28 as he blessed him: "May God give you of the dew of heaven, and of the fatness of the earth, and an abundance of grain and new wine."

The blessings of life are from God. In every recorded blessing in the Old Testament, the child's relationship with God is prominent. Therefore, the blessing must include a spiritual vision.

Our children cannot make it without God. God help us if our primary vision for our kids is educational, athletic, or social, instead of spiritual. Some parents make a huge deal about putting their kids to bed at night. I've done that quite a bit, but what I have done far more often is slipped into their rooms after they were asleep, knelt beside their beds, and prayed that God would use their lives to bring glory to Himself. We need to be pouring a spiritual vision into our children. We don't want them to just get by; we want them to be the super conquerors that Christ Jesus created them to be.

5. PROSPEROUS VISION

Isaac's vision of prosperity for his son is found in Genesis 27:28-29. It is not biblical to pray for our kids to be wealthy. But, by the same token, it is not biblical to seek poverty for our children either. We need to pray that our kids will be prosperous in this world, that they will rise up and be successful by kingdom standards and be stewards of what they have for Christ's kingdom.

I think the key word in verse 29 is *master*. "Be master of your brothers." Pray that your kids will master the opposition, master their roles in life, and master their finances—not the reverse. That's what it means to cast a prosperous vision for our kids. It's not that the hardships and hassles and temptations of this world will not matter to them, but they will end up on top of all that, praising and thanking the God who made it possible.

"I will give them a heart to know me, that I am the LORD. They will be my people, and I will be their God" (Jer. 24:7, NIV).

Read Jeremiah 24:7 in the margin. Fill in the blanks below with your child's name and pray it for your loved one!

Lord, give _____ a heart to know You and to know that You are the Lord. Help me do my part Lord, so that _____ will be Your man/woman, and You will be _____'s God.

What Happens When the Blessing Is Withheld?

When parents withhold the blessing from their children, either through ignorance or selfishness, the children will be tempted to respond in several ways that can actually make matters worse.

As you read the different translations of Proverbs 29:18 in the margin, underline what results when children lack vision because of withheld blessing.

Some try to earn the blessing. This leads to destructive pursuits of approval. It's like chasing a carrot on a stick. "Maybe if I do this, Dad will think I'm great." "Maybe if I achieve this." "Maybe if I reach this goal."

Some search for the blessing elsewhere. Some pull back from their parents and move away. Some may even get violent. Studies indicate that the number one candidate for gangs and cults is a kid who did not receive the blessing from his or her parents.

Some withdraw into a world of isolation and loneliness. They pull back and shut down. It's almost as if their world comes to an end. Having been hurt by those from whom they most needed to receive love, they conclude that being alone is better than making oneself vulnerable to others and then being wounded when they don't come through.

Some people strike out in anger. Have you ever considered the degree to which high school and young adult aggression is the surfacing anger of parental neglect? Parents ask their kids, "Why are you acting like this?" Very few teens understand their own feelings well enough to truly answer that kind of question, but if they could you might hear, "Because I can't stand another day of seeking and failing to receive your approval. Because I find more love and affection in my peer group than I ever receive at home. Because winning your attention through disobedience is better

"Where there is no vision, the people perish" (Prov. 29:18, KJV).

"Where there is no vision, the people are unrestrained" (Prov. 29:18).

"Without revelation people run wild" (Prov. 29:18, HCSB).

than winning your apathy and distractedness by being a 'good kid.' " Many parents understand the transforming power of giving the blessing only when the damage of not offering it to their kids has already been done.

When the blessing is given, a child emerges into adulthood able to answer the three most important questions in life:

1. Who am I? (a question of identity)
2. Why am I here? (a question of security)
3. Where am I going? (a question of confidence)

With those questions answered, life can be very fulfilling and fruitful, but without them, an enormous amount of energy is diverted into all sorts of futile searches for the blessing.

How Do You Live Without the Blessing?

Maybe you are having a hard time relating the truths to your children because you didn't receive the blessing from your parents. Maybe you are wondering how people are supposed to live without the blessing and then give it to their kids. Let me suggest two things that will bring incredible results in your life.

Hearing Your Spiritual Leaders

God can provide spiritual leaders—spiritual fathers and mothers—to pick up the slack left by our earthly parents. Those of you who are mature in the Lord and have already received the blessing have a responsibility to share it with others. It's not just about your own children.

Hearing Your Heavenly Father

At the end of the day, what really matters is what God says about you. He loves you and wants to minister to you.

Receive this word from your Heavenly Father, "This is My beloved [child], in whom I am well-pleased." Allow God to speak that truth into your life.

Read Zephaniah 3:17 in the margin. If someone were to ask God how He felt about you, what would He say?

_____

"The LORD your God is with you, he is mighty to save. He will take great delight in you, he will quiet you with his love, he will rejoice over you with singing" (Zeph. 3:17, NIV).

---

1. For much of this material, I am indebted to ideas contained in Gary Smalley and John Trent's, *The Blessing* (Nashville, TN: Thomas Nelson Publishers, 1986).

Before the Session

If you followed the "Before the Session" suggestion last week, display the "Blessing" placard as well as the previous weeks' placard.

During the Session

1. Ask: *What do we mean when we say something or someone has blessed us?* OR Show the ending of a movie where a father and adult son are reconciled (clean sports movies are good, such as "The Rookie." See note in the "To the Leader" section in the margin.) Invite the class to share other movies that have similar tear-jerker endings. Ask why those aging parent/adult child reunions get people all choked up. Point out that we can all relate with that child because no matter our age, we all long for our parents' blessing. FOR EITHER OPTION Ask: *Why do you think Dr. MacDonald said* blessing *is an essential healing word that will transform our families?*

2. Explain that "blessing" is a biblical concept—actually a very important family ritual. In story-fashion, summarize Genesis 27:1-29. Discuss the first activity of Day 1 (p. 19). Lead the class to share ways children of all ages—young child, teenager, and adult—ask for their parent's blessing. Ask why we all have such a need for parental blessing. (Read the quotation in the margin of Day 1, p. 20.) Discuss the second activity of Day 1. Ask: *How can we bless children even when we're not too pleased with them? What if you don't have children, how does this lesson apply to you? How might we as a class bless children in our church and community?*

3. Request that a volunteer read aloud Genesis 27:26-27. Ask participants to share two ways Isaac bestowed a blessing on his son. [Touch and spoken word] Ask why touch is so meaningful. Discuss excuses people give for not touching their children and why those excuses are so lame. Inquire: *What are appropriate ways to touch children in blessing if they are: a young child, a teenager, an adult? What are appropriate ways to bestow blessing through touch to children who aren't ours? What are appropriate ways to bless one another in this class through touch?*

To the Leader:

The Federal Copyright Act of 1976 stipulates special permission must be granted for any public performance of a movie—including showing a short clip in a Sunday School class! If your church does not already have permission, check with a church staff member about purchasing a Christian Video Licensing International at *www.cvli.com* or 1-888-771-CVLI (2854).

4. Discuss the first activity of Day 3 (p. 23). Request that the class give examples of spirit-crushing words. Ask: *Why would parents ever speak crushing words? What kinds of words are we to speak instead?* Encourage participants to give examples of life-giving words. Discuss the second activity. Explain: *All our words should build up and benefit children. Does that mean we always say words kids want to hear? How can we use words to discipline children yet still build them up and not crush them?* Encourage participants to be generous with life-giving words of blessing.

5. Discuss the first activity of Day 4 (p. 25). Ask the class to explain how literally smelling a child can affirm his or her value. Allow volunteers to share ways they have let their children know what a valuable gift they are, or share how their parents affirmed (and still affirm) their value. Inquire: *What kinds of visions do parents have for their children? How can some parental visions be more of a curse than a blessing? What kind of vision do we want to pour into our children?* Acknowledge: *All parents want their children to be happy and financially secure, but what true vision of prosperity needs to be instilled in our children?* Discuss the last paragraph of Day 4 (p. 26).

6. Option—if time permits, read Genesis 48:9-16. Lead the class to identify the five steps of blessing in Jacob's blessing of his grandsons.

7. Ask: *What happens when the blessing is withheld? How does the failure to give children a vision actually result in a type of death?* Acknowledge that we might not be able to specifically answer the three vital questions in Day 5 (p. 28) for all children, but lead the class to explore what basic answers children should be able to give to each question.

8. Ask: *How can adults bless children if they never received a parental blessing? How can this class share the blessing with one another?* Discuss the final activity of Day 5. Why is it so important to hear and believe what God says about you? Close in prayer, thanking God for His blessing.

After the Session

If the class determined ways they wanted to work together to bless children in your church and community (Step 2), enlist a volunteer to organize this ministry opportunity.

Honor

day One

A Universal Command

"Honor your father and your mother, that your days may be prolonged in the land which the LORD your God gives you" (Ex. 20:12). *Honor* is a very important concept in Scripture. In Deuteronomy 5:16, the Fifth Commandment is repeated with an expanded blessing: "Honor your father and your mother, as the LORD your God has commanded you, that your days may be prolonged and that it may go well with you on the land which the LORD your God gives you."

So significant was this commandment that the apostle Paul, under the inspiration of the Spirit of God, repeated it in his Letter to the Ephesians: "Honor your father and mother (which is the first commandment with a promise), so that it may be well with you, and that you may live long on the earth" (6:2-3). This is a command for all people in all periods of history.

Read Mark 7:5-13 in your Bible. What did Jesus declare about the religious leaders of His day?

_____

Why did He say that about them? _____

_____

If you have parents, you are to honor them no matter how old you may be. We never outgrow this command. In our day, we place a higher premium upon honoring self at the expense of those around us who need and deserve to be honored. We must remember that this is a commandment.

Honoring our parents is an action of deep sincerity. Far more than surface flattery, biblical honor involves identifying the things your parents have done right and praising them for those things.

All children are commanded to honor their parents—even if the parents did a lousy job. In the Old Testament Law, God reveals His heart toward people who don't honor their parents. "He who strikes his father or his mother shall surely be put to death"; and "He who curses his father or his mother shall surely be put to death" (Ex. 21:15,17).

I said some things to my parents in my foolish high school years that I greatly regret. Maybe you have too. I am so glad we don't live in the Old Testament time period or some of us wouldn't be here. But that is still God's heart. That's how God feels about anyone who would make the choice to dishonor his or her parents. It's extremely serious!

I do want to be really clear because I know some people have hurtful relationships with their parents. Honoring your parents does *not* mean:

1. *groveling and seeking their approval.* God wants us to be free from bondage to anyone's approval but His. The Apostle Paul said, "If I were still trying to please men, I would not be a bond-servant of Christ" (Gal. 1:10).

2. *making yourself vulnerable to their hurtful behavior.* Grown children can choose appropriate boundaries between themselves and their parents.

3. *ignoring or denying the past.* God's purposes are not advanced when we act as though certain issues do not exist. But forgiveness demands that those issues not influence your attitude toward your parents.

Honoring your parents *does* mean:

1. *choosing to place great value on your relationship with them and knocking off the attitude that "it doesn't matter."* It matters to God, and it should matter to you.

2. *taking the initiative to improve the relationship in whatever increments you can.*

3. *recognizing they have done some things right.* You might be thinking, *My parents didn't do anything right!* Your perspective is clouded, perhaps by great pain. But they did something right. If you open your heart to this truth, God will show you.

4. *acknowledging the sacrifices they have made for you.*

5. *seeing them as Christ does, with compassion and mercy.*

6. *forgiving them, even as God in Christ has forgiven you.*

Tomorrow we'll talk about the benefit of honoring our parents.

List things your parents did right and the sacrifices they made for you.

_____

_____

day Two

A Blessing to Us

What is the twofold reason we should honor our parents? (Hint: look back at Ephesians 6:2-3 in Day 1.)

1. _____

2. _____

Some people think it's wrong to obey God for their own benefit. Not so! If it were wrong, God would not have written the benefits of obedience into Scripture. God often motivates His children by promising to bless them. If God goes out of His way to record for us the benefits of obeying a certain command, it is not wrong to desire those benefits. Doesn't every decision of obedience bring blessing? God uses that to encourage us to live for Him.

WHAT'S THE BLESSING?

Let's look at the benefits of honoring our parents more closely: "that it may be well with you." What kind of promise is this? Is it health? Is it wealth? Is it safety? Is it an easier life? Is it relational favor with God? I don't know exactly what it means. I don't know what the blessings are that come from choosing to honor your parents. But the Bible says good things are going to happen. It could be that God will bless you at your point of greatest need if you obey the command to honor your parents.

Here's the second blessing phrase: "that you may live long on the earth." That's more specific, isn't it? The first and most obvious meaning of this phrase is that those who honor their parents will live longer than those who don't.

In your opinion, why would people who honor their parents live longer? _____

_____

Medical studies confirm that people who off-load bitterness, negativity, and unforgiveness experience better health. If you choose to sin, you choose to suffer. God's Word is very clear about that, so it shouldn't surprise us that a person who pursues obedience at every level is healthier, happier, and lives longer.

But if we look a little deeper, I think God is promising even more than a longer life for the one who chooses to obey. I believe this is also a promise about your legacy. In the family that chooses to honor the parents, there is a ripple effect that goes on for many years. When I honor my parents, my kids see something modeled; they will likely then choose to honor me, and through them the blessing of my obedience can continue into the third and fourth generations.

You say, "I don't think my parents honored their parents." Drive a stake in the ground right now. Maybe they didn't know what you know. Just say, "As for my family, things are going to be different." If you honor your parents, your kids will notice, and the influence of your life can continue for many generations.

Read Exodus 20:6 (a promise in the middle of the Ten Commandments). What will your descendants experience because of your choice to obey God?

_____

How many of your family's generations will be influenced by your obedience to God's law?

_____

The Story of David and Absalom

The story of David and Absalom (2 Sam. 13–19) illustrates vividly that when we don't honor our parents, it devastates them. When Absalom killed his half brother as revenge for the rape of his sister, Tamar, the family began to break down rapidly. David was so angry with Absalom that he fled the city of Jerusalem to avoid his father's wrath. Absalom spent three years in exile and had no contact with his father. Wouldn't you think David would be filled with rage and hatred toward his son during this time of banishment?

Look in your Bible at 2 Samuel 13:39 and 14:1. What was David's attitude toward his son Absalom?

_____

I'm thinking, "Dude, you're the king! If you want to go be with Absalom, go be with him!" But David was like, "I want to be with him, but I am so angry at him." David hated his son's actions, but still there remained that deep love that exists between members of the same family.

Maybe a similar situation exists in your family this very moment. Maybe you have been "banished" by your parents and wrongly assume that they do not love you.

David finally overcame his negative feelings enough to call for his son to come home. Picture the scene. As soon as Absalom gets back to Jerusalem, you would expect some big party, right? Wrong!

Read 2 Samuel 14:24,28.

What was David's condition for Absalom's return?

_____

How long did that last? _____

The king's son is living in the same city, and he doesn't see his own father for two more years! Frustrated, Absalom says, "Why have I come from Geshur? It would be better for me still to be there. Now therefore, let me see the king's face" (v. 32). This is such a vivid illustration of the mixed messages we often send in our own families.

Cite examples of mixed messages that are being sent in your family—perhaps by you.

_____

_____

Finally, David allowed Absalom to come in: "He came to the king and prostrated himself on his face to the ground before the king, and the king kissed Absalom" (v. 33).

More about this relationship tomorrow!

day Four

More Trouble Ahead

You might think that from here on everything was headed in a good direction in this father/son relationship. Not so! Second Samuel 15 tells us that Absalom went out and stirred up trouble.

Read 2 Samuel 15:1-4. How did Absalom dishonor his

father? _____

"In this manner Absalom dealt with all Israel who came to the king for judgment; Absalom stole away the hearts of the men of Israel" (2 Sam. 15:6).

The son, rejected for five years but now reconciled to his father, still had so much anger in his heart that he pulled the nation away from his dad. It became so bad for King David that he had to flee the city of Jerusalem.

David was devastated by Absalom and this group of conspirators.

Read 2 Samuel 15:30. How did David demonstrate his

devastation? _____

Once he was outside the city, some members of his army came to him and said, "We are going to take the kingdom back. We can win this! We can get the throne back for you, David." So David said, "Go get the throne back and win the battle, but don't hurt Absalom."

"Don't worry," they said. "We won't hurt him—we're going to kill him!" David threatened anyone who would touch him.

"What are you talking about? This treacherous so-called son of yours—why are you being so protective?"

David's only answer was "Don't hurt him. Don't hurt him" (see 2 Sam. 18:1–5).

So what happens? The battle is fought, and Absalom is killed. When a messenger arrives with news from the battle, the first words out of David's mouth are, "Is it well with the young man Absalom?" (2 Sam. 18:29). All David cares about is whether his son is OK. Soon a second messenger appears. Again, the first question out of David's mouth is, "Is it well with the young man Absalom?" (v. 32). The messenger shared the news that Absalom was dead. David was devastated again.

Read 2 Samuel 18:33–19:4. What is the most heart-wrenching part of this scene to you?

_____

So bizarre is this love/hate scene that Joab, the former commander of David's army, spoke out about it in 2 Samuel 19:5-6. Read this passage in the margin.

Is that unbelievable? Joab says, "You are messed up so bad! We went out to get the whole kingdom back for you, and you are more upset about your one son who died than all of the people who died (and could have died) in seeking to win the kingdom back for you!"

Here is the point. The relationship between a father and a son, between a mother and daughter, is so powerful that no negative circumstance can ever break that bond. In some ways your relationship with your parents is like

"Today you have covered with shame the faces of all your servants, who today have saved your life and the lives of your sons and daughters, the lives of your wives, and the lives of your concubines, by loving those who hate you, and by hating those who love you. For you have shown today that princes and servants are nothing to you; for I know this day that if Absalom were alive and all of us were dead today, then you would be pleased" (2 Sam. 19:5-6).

the one David had with Absalom. There is a very strong mixture of love and frustration that causes people to act in ways that may be very different from what they truly feel. If that cycle is to be broken, someone has to go first.

I am challenging you, as a follower of Jesus Christ, to step up to the plate. Just as there is within the heart of every child a longing for the blessing, so there is within the heart of every parent a longing to be honored and recognized for the love that has been given.

"When I was a child, I used to speak like a child, think like a child, reason like a child; when I became a man, I did away with childish things" (1 Cor. 13:11). Putting away childish things includes learning to see my parents from an adult's perspective, not from a child's perspective. Deep within every parent's heart—whether he or she can articulate it or not—is a longing for the day when one's precious child comes around the corner and says, "You really did love me. I am so sorry for all the grief I gave you. You didn't do everything perfectly, but you were a good dad! You were a good mom!" Those are adult words, mature words. They recognize the parent's love and give true honor.

> "Just as there is within the heart of every child a longing for the blessing, so there is within the heart of every parent a longing to be honored and recognized for the love that has been given."
> —James MacDonald

Reread Step 2 for honoring your parents from Day 1 (p. 32). It's time to start implementing some of those increments. What step to honor your parents will you take today?
❑ **Mow their lawn**
❑ **Call just to say hi.**
❑ **E-mail a picture of the grandchildren**
❑ **Other:** _____

day Five

It's Time to Honor Our Parents

Clearly, this is something that God Himself wants communicated. It is time to honor our parents …

1. *even if we don't feel like it.* That is part of becoming adults. We do lots of things we don't feel like doing. How many times have our moms

and dads done things they didn't feel like doing? Maybe you feel angry or hurt or neglected or misunderstood by your parents. It's time to get past those things. As children, we must honor our parents because raising kids is an exhausting process, because kids often bring a lot of pain into their parents' lives that we fail to see, and because our kids will soon grow up to treat us the way we treated our parents.

When we communicate to our parents through word or deed that they do not hold a place of honor in our lives and schedules, we have committed a great sin. First Timothy 5:8 says, "If anyone does not provide for his own, and especially for those of his household, he has denied the faith and is worse than an unbeliever." That provision is to be far more than financial. It should involve the giving of our time and emotional energy also.

Does the thought that your kids will treat you the way you treated your parents bring you:
❏ **Comfort** or ❏ **Consternation**   **Why?**

_____

2. *even if they won't receive it.* You may be thinking, *If I were to try to honor my parents, they wouldn't hear me. I can already hear the door slamming or the phone hanging up.* That is what the prodigal son was thinking (Luke 15). When he came to the end of his funds and the beginning of his senses, he decided, "I'm just going to live in the barn. I'll be my dad's slave." And as he made his way home, he was nervous that his dad was going to reject him.

Read Luke 15:20-24 in your Bible. How did the father respond to the son's efforts at reconciliation?

_____

You may be surprised how receptive your parents are. Besides, we don't do what we do for the response. We do it because we believe God's Word and want to obey Him.

You know that I believe in both a crisis and a process in all matters of transformation. The process of honoring our parents is done in a thousand

> "We don't do what we do for the response. We do it because we believe God's Word and want to obey Him."
> – James MacDonald.

little things over time, but the crisis is essential to jump-start that process. As a crisis for honoring your parents, I recommend Dennis Rainey's idea of writing a formal tribute.[1] In a written tribute, you can acknowledge all the good your parents have done for you. Tell them how thankful you are to be their son or daughter. Express your love for them and recognize their sacrifices on your behalf.

GETTING STARTED

Here are some practical ideas to get you started:

1. *Be honest.* Don't say a bunch of slobbery things you don't mean. You don't have to pretend that you approve of everything your parents do or that they are perfect.

2. *Be positive.* Just focus on the good. Philippians 4:8 says, "Whatever is true, whatever is honorable, whatever is right, whatever is pure, whatever is lovely, whatever is of good repute … dwell on these things." Focus on the good—whatever it is. If you can't see it, pray and ask the Lord for wisdom. He will show it to you.

3. *Be public.* Do this in front of your spouse and children, if possible. God will use it to spread a legacy of honor throughout your family.

4. *Be decisive.* Don't put it off. The time is now.

Seek to honor your parents every chance you have. Step out by faith and write a tribute. Regardless of the response, God will bless you.

Write a tribute on a separate sheet of paper. Use the suggestions given in this week's study or follow the prompts below:

Dear Mom and Dad,

Thank you for being my parents.
I appreciate:
One of my favorite memories of you is:
I love you.

---

1. Dennis Rainey with David Boehl, *The Tribute and the Promise* (Nashville: Thomas Nelson, 1994).

Before the Session

1. If you followed the "Before the Session" suggestion in Week 1, display the "Honor" placard as well as the previous weeks' placards.
2. Be prepared to share any specifics about your class ministry opportunity you discussed in Week 2.
3. Read carefully 2 Samuel 13–19.
4. For each participant, make a strip of beige paper with a black line drawn lengthwise through the center.

During the Session

1. Ask: *What does it mean to honor someone? If you had no limits, what one person would you honor, how would you honor him or her, and why?* OR Organize the class into two groups. Ask Group 1 to compile a list of the top 10 things kids do to irritate their parents. Ask Group 2 to compile a list of the top 10 things parents do to irritate their kids. After groups have time to work, invite them to share their lists. Acknowledge that parents and children don't always see eye to eye, yet God has firm commands about how children are to relate to their parents. FOR EITHER OPTION Invite participants to turn in their Bibles to God's "Top 10 List" in Exodus 20. Ask them to read number 5 on His list (20:12). Ask at what age children are expected to obey this command.

2. Ask: *What does honoring your parents* not *mean?* Using the principles from Mark 7 and the discussion in Day 1, explore what biblical honor means. Allow volunteers to share their responses to the final activity of Day 1 (p. 33).

3. Discuss the first activity of Day 2. Request that participants explain why they agree or disagree that it's OK to obey God's law because they will benefit by doing so. Ask: *Why do you think this was the first of God's commandments that came with a promise? What do you think the phrase "that it may be well with you" means?* (Assure adults there isn't always one right answer for every question; "honor" your participants' intelligence by asking challenging questions that require thought and discussion.)

To the Leader:

These past three weeks of study may have been difficult for some of your class participants. Write them a note, honoring them for their dedication and faithfulness to studying and applying God's Word.

Discuss the second and third activities of Day 2 (p. 34). Ask: *How can honoring your parents as an adult actually transform your family?*

4. Acknowledge that many children, in a childish rage, will declare they hate their parents. Ask participants who are parents how they felt when their children made that declaration or dishonored them in some way. Ask: *Do you think our older parents are any less devastated when we dishonor them? Why?* Summarize the story of David and Absalom from Genesis 13–18, asking participants to share answers to the activities in Days 3 and 4 to gain an understanding of the love/hate relationship between this father and son.

5. Ask: *What was Dr. MacDonald's point in relating the story of David and Absalom? We've been told in past sessions that we as parents may need to break some destructive cycles in our families. Who is Dr. MacDonald challenging to break the negative cycles that may exist between us and our parents?* Request that someone read 1 Corinthians 13:11 (p. 38). Inquire: *What childish things might we say or think that keep us from honoring our parents? We're grown now, how can we put away those childish things?*

6. Ask what might keep Christian adults from honoring their parents. Ask: *What does Dr. MacDonald say we are to do anyway?* (See Day 5.) *How might our parents surprise us if we choose to honor them? Now that you are a parent, how do you understand and appreciate your own parents— warts and all?* Allow volunteers to share little and big things they do to honor their parents.

7. Ask participants if they have ever presented a written tribute to their parents, and, if so, how their parents responded. Urge them to complete their written tribute and pray about how and when to present it to their parents.

8. Acknowledge that some participants may not have grown up in healthy families where they experienced forgiveness, blessing, and honor. Distribute the strips of paper you prepared before the session and ask participants to consider it their line in the sand. Starting today they are going to live the healing words of forgiveness, blessing, and honor within their families. Encourage them to keep their "line" as a visible reminder of their commitment. Close in prayer.

Truth

day One

What Is Truth?

On what are you basing your judgments? What system of belief is informing the decisions you make and the actions you take? If you are not building your life on truth, then you are headed for a big-time crash no matter how sincere your intentions may be.

Jesus said, "Sanctify them in the truth; Your word is truth" (John 17:17). The word *sanctify* means change. It is God's transforming process in the life of every believer. What gas is to a motor, what gunpowder is to a fireworks display, what good food is to our bodies, truth is to transformation.

If you want to see change in your life and in your family, you must take hold of this matter of truth.

According to John 17:17, where is truth found?
❑ **Science**   ❑ **Evening News**
❑ **Space**   ❑ **God's Word**

Every word that proceeds from the mouth of God is absolute, authoritative, binding truth.

Do you want a strong family? Do you want a marriage that is going to make it to the finish line? Do you want kids who are going to rise up and call you blessed? That's what most desire but few get because their foundation is wrong. They may invest a lot of time and energy in building their family, but if the foundation is wrong, it only takes a little storm before everything they've worked for comes crashing down. Jesus tells a story to make this important point (see Matt. 7:24-27 printed in the margin).

There are two kinds of families. There are families building on the rock, and families building on the sand; families building on truth, and families building on … ? There are some pretty attractive things about

"Everyone who hears these words of Mine and acts on them, may be compared to a wise man who built his house on the rock. And the rain fell, and the floods came, and the winds blew and slammed against that house; and yet it did not fall, for it had been founded on the rock. Everyone who hears these words of Mine and does not act on them, will be like a foolish man who built his house on the sand. The rain fell, and the floods came, and the winds blew and slammed against that house; and it fell—and great was its fall" (Matt. 7:24-27).

43

building your home on the sand. It's fast, it looks good on the outside, and your neighbors will be really impressed. "Sand castles" free up a lot of time for other stuff that brings more instant gratification.

On the other hand, building your house on the rock—the truth— requires intentionality and focus.

Look again at Matthew 7:24. How do you build your house—your family—on the rock?

_____

It seems like a big hassle: lots of time and effort to drill deep and build carefully upon the truth. And worst of all, until a major storm hits, it looks like the house built on truth was a lot of wasted effort.

Two kinds of families, but only one kind of experience. "The rain fell, and the floods came, and the winds blew and slammed against that house." What family can you think of that has not encountered storms? Your family is going to have some storms just as mine will. Only when the storms rage does it become apparent which families are built on the rock of truth, and which ones are built on the sand.

Two kinds of families, one kind of experience. two kinds of outcomes. The house on the sand had a great fall—total, sudden devastation. The house founded on the rock stood. Strong families are built on the truth. If that seems like a small thing to you, I assure you it is not. When your marriage is over, when your kids are living in the world, when your finances are in ruin, when your spiritual life has crashed to the ground—it's the worst kind of pain a person can experience. This week we'll be look at teachings from God's Word on how to avoid that pain by building your family on the truth.

Write your last name on the foundation upon which your family is built right now.

The _____ Family   The _____ Family
     ROCK   SAND

Truth Requires Diligence

In 2 Timothy, the apostle Paul was writing to a young pastor named Timothy about building his ministry. By application, these truths also have much to say about building strong families.

Look at 2 Timothy 2:14-15 in the margin. What prevailing action and attitude did Paul urge Timothy to display?

_____

Diligence is essential to building your family on the truth, but what kind of diligence?

DILIGENCE TO AVOID FOOLISH ISSUES

"Remind them of these things, and solemnly charge them." Charge them how? "In the presence of God." The idea here is that we are not alone. Almighty God Himself is with us and is very intent on this message. He wants us all to hear it.

Read 2 Timothy 2:14-15 again and underline what parents are to diligently charge their families to do.

I wonder if there is anything that brings such devastation to our homes as wrangling about words. That word *wrangle* could be translated literally "a war of words." It's the silly, nonsensical, back-and-forth-and-back-and-forth arguing and blah, blah, blah of life. Silly, secondary issues that are not substantive or significant and that ought not be tearing our homes apart.

We only get so many words in our families. The older our kids get, the fewer words we have with them. What are you going to spend your words on? I fear we're wasting our words on issues of little value, and then we're too exhausted to pour into our families the kind of truth that can be a

"Remind them of these things, and solemnly charge them in the presence of God not to wrangle about words, which is useless and leads to the ruin of the hearers. Be diligent to present yourself approved to God as a workman who does not need to be ashamed, accurately handling the word of truth" (2 Tim. 2:14-15).

fountain of life to them. Instead, let's choose words of truth that build and guide and establish a foundation of wisdom that will last a lifetime.

God, give us the humility to go back to our children or spouse and say, "I am sorry. I have been pressing you about a matter that is not significant." We must have diligence to avoid foolish issues if we are going to build on the truth.

Have you been majoring on minor issues? ❑ Yes ❑ No

If so, what are they, and what are you going to do

about it?_____

_____

DILIGENCE TO PRIORITIZE THE WORD OF TRUTH

"Be diligent to present yourself approved to God as a workman who does not need to be ashamed, accurately handling the word of truth" (2 Tim. 2:15). This is not a message to apply next year, or next month, or even next week. This is a message for today, for right now.

"Present yourself approved to God" regarding the Word of Truth. God knows how you are handling His Book. He knows whether you are attentive to it and leading your family by it or whether you are digging it out and dusting it off for church on Sunday—or maybe not even that. It really matters!

Each of us needs to be "a workman who does not need to be ashamed." If the truth were known, a lot of God's people are ashamed about their avoidance or ignorance of the Word of Truth. You say, "I hardly even know what the Bible says." Why don't you know? There are things that are happening in your home and with your children that are not right. We don't want to be ashamed by the way we handle the Word of Truth.

"Accurately handling the word of truth." When I was a kid, I memorized this verse in the King James Version as "rightly dividing the word of truth." We are supposed to be cutting it straight, rightly dividing, accurately handling the Word of Truth. No longer will you allow yourself the luxury of wandering from what the Word of God says. You are accurately handling the Word of Truth and making it a priority.

"Choose words of truth that build and guide and establish a foundation of wisdom that will last a lifetime."
—James MacDonald

"Set a guard, O LORD, over my mouth; Keep watch over the door of my lips" (Ps. 141:3).

Read Deuteronomy 32:46-47 in your Bible. Why is it essential to handle God's Word accurately?

_____

Truth Requires Correction

You say, "If I take a stand like you described, there is going to be conflict!" That cannot be avoided, because building your family on truth requires correction.

Read 2 Timothy 2:24-25 in the margin and complete this statement.
If I am going to build my family on truth, I must:

_____

"The Lord's bond-servant must not be quarrelsome, but be kind to all, able to teach, patient when wronged, with gentleness correcting those who are in opposition" (2 Tim. 2:24-25).

Those words "with gentleness" are so important. When we pursue truth with gentleness, we safeguard our homes against harsh, brutal words that are really just thinly veiled personal hurt or frustration with a family member's problems. "With gentleness correcting those who are in opposition."

A decision to diligently pursue truth in your home will bring opposition. First, the opposition of *misunderstanding*. If you build your family on the truth, there is going to be some rejection. You may be accused of being harsh, no matter how loving you have been, simply because the Word of Truth cuts. You may have people judge your motives or attack your character, pointing out that, "You're not perfect yourself."

There will be the opposition of *tiredness*. "I am so tired from constantly teaching and training my kids in the truth," you say. "At times they seem to need an unending stream of correction, and it is exhausting!" Don't let the opposition of tiredness stop you from doing what's right.

Then there's the opposition of *emotional distance*. Perhaps you have teenagers who call you uncool and unloving, and they won't see for many years the value of the truths on which you are building your family and refusing to compromise. Don't back down, no matter how many hurtful words they say or rolled eyes you must endure. In the major things, do what's right even if it sets off a war in your home. Draw the line. When your kids become adults and are raising their own kids, they will know you did what was best for them. Someday they will thank you.

Parent or teacher, are you bone-tired of leading, building, and correcting the children in your charge? What encouragement can you gain from Galatians 6:9?

STANDING WHERE IT'S HARDEST

You are not standing for the truth unless you are doing so at the specific point where the truth is being resisted. This is absolutely critical. You can be standing for the truth in 15 different places, but if you are conceding at the very point of opposition, you are not building your home on the truth. It only takes one leak to create a flood of compromise.

What is that point of opposition in your home right now? Where is the battle raging?
❏ **Dress (modesty issues)**
❏ **Entertainment (morality Issues)**
❏ **Relationships (manners Issues)**
❏ **Spending (money issues)**
❏ **Other:** _____

Stand firm at that place. You say, "There's going to be conflict." Then have it! That is the exact place where the Word of Truth needs to come to bear upon your home.

Why do we stand on the truth? Why go through such potential hardship? Because it is only when we stand on the truth that we work in partnership with God. Notice what it says in verse 25: "With gentleness correcting those who are in opposition, if perhaps God may grant them repentance leading to the knowledge of the truth." When you wield the truth, then you are in partnership with God. When you get truth on the table, then God may grant them repentance. That's the first step in all change—genuine repentance—and only God can produce it.

Unless you are brokering truth, God is not supporting the investments you are making in your family relationships.

Truth Requires Relationship

You say, "Truth seems cold and separated from relationship." On the contrary, building your family on truth demands loving, meaningful relationships.

Paul discussed the connection between truth and family relationships in 2 Timothy 3:14–16. First, there must be a relationship with the learner. "You, however, continue in the things you have learned and become convinced of, knowing from whom you have learned them" (v. 14).

> **Paul said, "Keep going in the things you've learned because of ..." Underline your answer.**
> **What you've learned**
> **Why you've learned**
> **From whom you've learned**

Paul says, "Do you know what's really important? It's the relationship." What matters most is not what or how or why Timothy learned—it's who did the teaching that was paramount.

Paul wasn't talking about himself teaching Timothy, because in the beginning of the next verse he references Timothy's childhood: "Knowing from whom you have learned them, and that from childhood you have known the sacred writings."

> **Read 2 Timothy 1:5 in the margin and underline who taught Timothy.**

That ought to encourage every single parent. Timothy's father was Greek and apparently did not worship the God of Israel (Acts 16:1,3), but

"I am mindful of the sincere faith within you, which first dwelt in your grandmother Lois and your mother Eunice, and I am sure that it is in you as well" (2 Tim. 1:5).

Timothy had a faithful mother and grandmother who poured truth into his life. Truth is most powerfully taught in the context of relationship.

It is not your pastor's job to teach the Word of God to your kids. It is not the Sunday School teacher's or the youth worker's responsibility. Praise God for those supplemental things, but it is your job as a parent to teach your children the Word of God.

Parents, if you are getting that done, I want to encourage you. Even if your kids struggle, even if they wander, I believe with all of my heart that they are coming back. They won't stay away forever. The blessing will bring them back, and they will return to the truths that you have over many years poured into their hearts—provided you taught that truth in the context of a relationship.

Not only is it important to have a relationship with the learner, but also with the Author. Take note of what Paul says at the end of 2 Timothy 3:14–15: "Continue in the things you have learned and become convinced of, knowing from whom you have learned them, and that from childhood you have known the sacred writings which are able to give you the wisdom that leads to salvation through faith which is in Christ Jesus." At the end of the day, it's all about Jesus Christ. We do not worship the Bible. The Bible conveys the truth about Christ. From the Bible we learn about the Savior. Jesus said to the Pharisees in John 5:39, "You search the Scriptures because you think that in them you have eternal life; it is these that testify about Me."

It's all about Jesus Christ. It is essential that we remember this. All worship flows from knowing the Christ of Scripture. All comfort flows from knowing the Christ of God's Word. All grace and goodness and blessing and joy flow from knowing the Person who is revealed in the Book.

How is your relationship with the learners in your family? ❑ **Great**   ❑ **Needs Work**   ❑ **Terrible**

How's your relationship with the Author?
❑ **Great**   ❑ **Needs Work**   ❑ **Terrible**

Spend some time in prayer about your responses.

day *Five*

Families Built on Truth Prevail

Do you want to win the most important battle in life—the battle for your family? Do you want to get through the tough things you are facing right now? Get your family anchored on the truth.

Read 2 Timothy 3:16 in your Bible and answer the following:

What will the Word of God do in your family?

_____

Where did the Scriptures come from?

_____

God chose the very words of Scripture. "Men moved by the Holy Spirit spoke from God" (2 Pet. 1:21)—word for word from the heart of God.

All in favor of building our families on the truth? Let me give you 10 practical ideas. Fire these up in your home. If you are a single adult, then fire these up with your roommate.

1. Start a regular time of family Bible reading and prayer.
2. Memorize a portion of God's Word as a family. Psalm 127 or Ephesians 6 would be good places to start.
3. Have a contest to learn the books of the Bible.
4. Read through the Bible in a year.
5. Get a teaching series on the family. Sit down together, listen to the messages, make notes, pray about it, and discuss it.
6. Make decisions about family matters using the Bible. If you're facing a big decision, ask your pastor, "What passage can we read that will help us make this decision?"

7. Turn off the television and read a Bible story out loud with enthusiasm! Let your children see that Mom and Dad are fired up about the truth that is in the Book.

8. Attend a Bible study or class together. Attend as a couple. Attend as a family. Learn from God's Word.

9. Don't just pray with your kids before bed, but read a portion of God's Word to them.

10. Choose some family values and post them at home. Our family has five family values painted in a beautiful mural on our family room wall where they are always before our eyes. Here they are (feel free to use them or create your own):

- *Love God.* "Love the Lord your God with all your heart" (Mark 12:30).
- *Family first.* Loyalty, commitment, unity, vision.
- *Work hard.* What a great vision to give our children in this lazy, selfish world—work hard!
- *Tell the truth.* Even when it's painful. Even when it's going to get you into more trouble.
- *Be kind.* Treat others the way you want to be treated.

What family values would you like to represent your family? List them here.

_____

_____

_____

Why should you do all this? Read 2 Timothy 3:17 in your Bible and fill in the blanks:

So that I, my spouse, and my children may be

_____ _____ for every good work.

God's Word contains all the truth we need to be thoroughly equipped for the voyage of life.

Before the Session

1. If you followed the "Before the Session" suggestion in Week 1, display the "Truth" placard as well as the previous weeks' placards.

2. Enlist five volunteers to be prepared to read Matthew 6:31-33; Matthew 19:6; 2 Corinthians 6:14; Philippians 4:8; and Colossians 3:17 (for Step 5).

3. Prepare a large writing surface (board, poster, etc.) for use during the session.

During the Session

1. Invite participants to share examples of people who were sincere but sincerely wrong. [Examples: Darwin; early scientists who thought earth was the center of the universe and bloodletting was the cure for diseases; Islamic radicals] OR Ask participants to share the absolute essentials they would look for in a house they were building or buying. Write responses on the board. Be sure to include "solid foundation." Ask: *What good are the "extras" in a house if the foundation is unstable? Why?* Compare building a home/family to building a house. FOR EITHER OPTION Read Psalm 127:1. Explain that there are parents who sincerely want to build a strong home for their children, but the way they're going about it is sincerely wrong. Every strong home builds on a stable foundation.

2. Explain that every adult who wants to be transformed must address the probing questions Dr. MacDonald asks at the beginning of Day 1 (p. 43). Ask someone to read that first paragraph. Request that participants turn to John 18:38 in their Bibles and share the question Pilate asked Jesus. Ask: *Do people still ask that question? What are some answers they might be getting?* Discuss the first activity of Day 1. Ask: *If we want to build strong families, what is the only true foundation upon which we can build?*

3. Request that a volunteer read Matthew 7:24-27. Write "Family #1" and "Family #2" over two columns on the board. As you lead the following discussion, write participants' responses in the appropriate column: *What two kinds of families are in Jesus' parable? What one experience*

To the Leader:

Does your family have core values? If not, make time to talk it over with your spouse and children and establish some this week. Share those core values with your class to encourage them to build their families on a written list of biblical values.

did they both have? What two different outcomes resulted? What kind of "sandy" foundations do some families build on? Discuss the second activity in Day 1. Explore why it is easier to build on the sand and what it takes to build a family on the solid rock of God's truth. (Let that lead into the Day 2 discussion of diligence.)

4. Discuss the first activity of Day 2 (p. 45). Explore the meaning of diligence. Discuss the second activity. Ask: *What benefit do we gain from wrangling about words? What results when we fail to charge our families—and ourselves—to stop this war of words? We're told not to sweat the small stuff, but how can we distinguish between minor issues that are foolish and issues that will grow into large problems if we don't nip them in the bud?*

5. Ask someone to read 2 Timothy 2:15. Ask: *How can we not be ashamed with how we have handled God's Word?* Discuss the last activity of Day 2 (p. 47). Inquire: *How might we give children the impression God's words are meaningless? How can we convey that God's Word is our life?* Explain that "rightly dividing" literally means "cutting straight." Explain that we must use God's Word to cut straight through tough issues with our families. Ask the class to listen for what marriage and child-rearing issues God's Word cuts through as the pre-enlisted volunteers read their assigned verses. Call for responses. Remind participants we must teach children truths from God's Word gently and never beat them over the head with the Bible.

6. Discuss the first activity of Day 3. Ask what parents will face when they speak truth in their homes. Invite volunteers to share which forms of opposition discussed in Day 3 they have faced. Discuss the third activity in Day 3 (p. 48). Evaluate the difference between majoring on minors and standing firm at the place where the battle is raging.

7. Discuss the first activity of Day 4. Discuss why relationship is so important in building homes on truth. Read Deuteronomy 6:6-7 and explore how that expresses relationship. Ask: *Whose job is it to teach our children God's Word? How can we use, but not solely depend on, the resources of our church to teach our families?* Allow volunteers to share which of the suggestions in Day 5 they already use in their homes. Urge participants to choose three suggestions to put in place in their homes. Discuss the final activity in Day 5 (p. 52). Close in prayer.

Church

Believe in the Church

Families are trying to become all they can be in the Lord. Yet many are doing so without the help of the only institution God created to nurture and support the family—the church.

Consider, for example, the material we covered last week on truth. What are the chances of building your family on the truth without meaningful connectedness to a Bible-believing, local church? A family left to itself cannot live out what God's Word teaches with any kind of consistency. That is why God has placed us in communities of faith called local churches.

Read 1 Timothy 3:15 in the margin. What is the relationship between the church and the truth?

_____

"I am writing you these instructions so that, if I am delayed, you will know how people ought to conduct themselves in God's household, which is the church of the living God, the pillar and foundation of the truth" (1 Tim. 3:15, NIV).

The church is the pillar of the truth. What does a pillar do? It holds up the roof. The church is also the foundation of the truth. It's a strong support that will allow the truth to stand in your home during times of hardship that shake your family to its very core.

As both the pillar and foundation of God's truth, the church must not be neglected in our families if we want to experience God's transforming power. The church of Jesus Christ is an incredible resource to help your marriage, train your children, and enlarge your family's capacity to receive all the blessings God wants to give.

This week I want to share three things to help you access the benefits of the church to change your family: (1) believe in the church, (2) submit to the church, and (3) participate in the church.

First, you have to believe in the church, like Jesus does.

Read Matthew 16:13-15 in your Bible (keep it open there for the rest of today's study). In what did Jesus seem to be most interested?
❑ **What people said about Him.**
❑ **What His disciples said about Him.**

Who do you say Jesus is? It doesn't matter who your mom thinks Jesus is, or who your grandpa thinks Jesus is, or who your neighbor thinks Jesus is. "Who do *you* think Jesus is?"

Jesus turned to the disciples and said, " 'Who do you say that I am?' "

Look at Matthew 16:16-17 and complete the following:

Simon Peter answered that _____

_____

Jesus declared Peter was blessed because _____

_____

How does a person come to know Christ personally? If you have turned from your sin and embraced Christ by faith as the only basis for your forgiveness, the only reason you even have a clue is because God pursued you. He opened your eyes, and all of a sudden you got it!

Why hasn't your coworker or next door neighbor gotten it? God hasn't opened his or her eyes yet. The Bible tells us, "The god of this world has blinded the minds of the unbelieving so that they might not see the light of the gospel of the glory of Christ" (2 Cor. 4:4). Jesus made it clear why Peter got it: "Flesh and blood did not reveal this to you, but My Father who is in heaven."

Then Jesus made this key statement about the church: "I also say to you that you are Peter, and upon this rock I will build My church" (Matt. 16:18).

What was the rock upon which Jesus would build His church?
❑ **The man, Peter**
❑ **Peter's confession of faith that Jesus is the Son of God**

Jesus said, "Hey, Peter, you are a little man who said a big thing! I am going to build My church on what you said." And isn't that exactly what has happened? The church of Jesus Christ has been built upon the fact that Jesus is not just a man, not simply a good moral teacher, but that He is the Christ, the Son of the living God.

day Two

He's Building His Church

Controversy around this Matthew passage has caused many people to miss two incredible statements about the church. Here is the first one: "I will build My church." Jesus Christ said He will build His church. Isn't that fantastic?

The word *church* comes from a compound word that means the called-out ones.

Read John 15:19 in your Bible. From what is the

church called out? _____

God said, "Come on out of the world! Leave your sin behind. It's taking you nowhere. Come over here! Be with Me. I am building a kingdom. You can be part of it." If you haven't heard that call, you can hear it today. Be reconciled to God through repentance and faith.

"We don't really believe in the church. My wife and I are really into Jesus, but we don't need the church thing." Have you ever heard that? Every time I do I want to say, "If you are really so 'into Jesus,' you oughta be into His church too, because He sure is."

"Christ also loved the church and gave Himself up for her" (Eph. 5:25).

Read Ephesians 5:25 in the margin. How much is Jesus

into His church? _____

Christ loves the church. If you love Christ, you have to love His church, because that is what He is all about in this world.

"If you love Christ, you have to love His church, because that is what He is all about in this world." —James MacDonald

You say, "We had a bad experience. We used to go to church, but we quit. We used to be involved, but now we are sort of sitting on the sidelines." Have you ever had a bad meal at a restaurant? Or have you ever gone to a store and been sold something and later thought, *Man, I got so ripped off!* You still eat at restaurants, don't you? Do you still buy things from stores? In the same way, I still believe in the church of Jesus Christ. I am not going to be turned off just because I've been hurt or wounded.

Jesus is for the church. Yes, it has sinful people in it, and it doesn't always work perfectly, but I believe in the church because Jesus promised, "I will build My church."

WE'RE GONNA WIN!

Look back at Matthew 16:18. What is the second important statement in that verse?

_____

We're gonna win! There is a desire within each of us to be part of something we know is headed in the right direction—something that's going to win. The Lord said, "The gates of hell will not prevail against My church." When you stand in heaven someday, you want to be able to say, "I was on the winning team! I poured all of my effort and all of my energy into the things Jesus said would succeed." If you want your family to win, get them in the middle of the church of Jesus Christ. It is going to prevail. Jesus promised it would.

With my whole heart I believe in the church of Jesus Christ. I believe in the blood-bought, born-again, Spirit-filled army of the redeemed, and I am so thankful that my family is growing together under that protective umbrella. Is yours?

The church of Jesus Christ is an incredible resource for your family—full of truth and relationships and fellowship and support and accountability. If you would march your family to the very center of this thing called the church, the odds of having a successful, God-honoring family would be much more in your favor.

**It has to start with you believing in the church.
Do you?** ❑ Yes ❑ No

Why? _____

Submit to the Church

"Obey your leaders and submit to them, for they keep watch over your souls as those who will give an account. Let them do this with joy and not with grief, for this would be unprofitable for you" (Heb. 13:17).

> **Read Titus 1:7-9 and 1 Peter 5:1-3 in your Bible. In the margin, record qualities that church leaders must possess and display.**

The Bible teaches that you and your family are to find leaders like that in a church and place yourselves under their care.

Unless they are asking you to sin or do something that would dishonor the Lord, you ought to do the things they are asking you to do. God will honor that, even if you don't see how at the moment.

When Scripture calls you to obey your leaders and submit to them, it is talking about obeying the things they teach you and the methods of ministry they call the church to implement. Consider how many hours you have spent sitting under the teaching of God's Word in your own church or how many hours you have spent reading Christian books that explain portions of God's Word and call you to align your life with it. What have you done with what you've heard? You must obey it; you must do the things you are taught—not based on human authority but based on the authority God has given to the leaders in the church.

> **Read Hebrews 13:17 again. Why should I submit to my church leaders?** ❑ For their sake ❑ For my sake

"They keep watch over your souls" (Heb. 13:17). Church leaders who take their roles seriously are carrying a huge load, and you are in a position to help them help you by doing the things they teach you to do with a willing, submissive heart.

"Let them [lead you] with joy and not with grief, for this would be unprofitable for you" (Heb. 13:17). Allow your church leaders to watch over you with joy. What makes a person a joy to lead? At our church, we call them FAT Christians. They are Faithful, Available, and Teachable.

Who gets the lion's share of the attention? The FAT Christians or the grief-causing Christians? Eventually, the church leaders begin to say (like Jesus did), "I think I am going to pour my energy into the faithful, available, teachable people. Church members who are a joy to lead will reap far more of the benefits Christ wants to give them through their church.

What kind of Christian are you in your church?
❏ **A FAT Christian** ❏ **A grief-causing Christian**

THE CHURCH—A GREAT BACKUP PLAN

You ask, "What does this have to do with my family?" If you're plugged into the life of the church, when the authority structure in your home fails, the authority structure in the church will be there to back it up. And make no mistake, the authority structure in the home does fail. If you're not plugged into the church, what are you going to do if a son or daughter goes off the deep end? What's your support system if you have a serious financial crisis or a conflict at home that cannot be resolved?

It can be a hassle at times having people involved in your life like that. Maybe you have had a few negative experiences at church, and you think your family would be better off without the accountability. If you think that, you are wrong. In spite of the occasional hassle my family gets at church, we are far better off than we would ever be without all the good we receive from the church. And if we ever get into a really tough spot as a family, I am thankful that our church will be there to back us up and make sure God's priorities are being advanced in our home.

Sometimes the church doesn't work perfectly, but it is an incredible blessing and a wonderful resource. It brings great joy; it provides much needed accountability; and it gives you connectedness. Get your family into the center of the church.

Pray for your church leaders and the heavy burden they carry. Ask God to make you a joy to lead. Commit to get your family involved in church.

day Four

Participate in the Church

This is the third, and perhaps most important, way to access the benefits of the church. In Hebrews 10, after celebrating the riches of Christ, the author writes, "Therefore, brethren, since we have confidence to enter the holy place by the blood of Jesus." The holy place is the place where God resides. We can come to Him because of the atoning work of Christ on the cross.

The author goes on to say, "We have confidence to enter the holy place by the blood of Jesus, by a new and living way which He inaugurated for us through the veil, that is, His flesh" (vv. 19-20). In Old Testament times, a veil separated people from the presence of God. When Christ died, the veil in the temple was torn in two. Now there is a new veil; it's Christ Himself. He is the way in.

DRAW NEAR

Read Hebrews 10:19-22 in your Bible. What are we to do since the veil has been torn?

Now read James 4:8 in the margin and underline what God promises to do if you draw near to Him.

"Draw near to God and He will draw near to you" (Jas. 4:8).

There is absolutely no barrier now between you and God. You have been washed clean. Isn't that a great thing? God loves you and has set His grace upon you. There is nothing that should hinder your capacity to express worship to God.

All biblical churches have as their centerpiece a weekend worship service where believers come together to connect with God. A weekly, corporate God encounter can do more to turn up the spiritual temperature in your family than anything else. Here are some things you can do to maximize your family's weekly worship:

1. *Come together.* Get ready for church together, arrive together, sit together, leave together, and discuss together what the Lord is doing in your hearts.

2. *Come often.* Come every week.

3. *Come early.*

4. *Come prepared.* Pray with your family before you come to church. Read a portion of Scripture. Stop in the driveway and say, "We're heading to worship God; let's get our hearts ready." Pray that the time of worship will be meaningful for your family.

Your children are watching you worship.

Check the statement below that best describes your worship. I am:

❑ **Fired up about God, enthused about the truth found in Him, worshiping in spirit and truth**

❑ **Distant, apathetic, and critical**

In either case, your nonverbals are sending a huge message to your kids. Do you want to participate in the life of the church? Do you want to bring your family to the center of the church? Worship Christ. Draw near with full assurance of faith.

We'll finish talking about participation in the church tomorrow.

day *Five*

Participate in the Church (Part 2)

To review where we've been and look ahead to where we're going, read Hebrews 10:19-25 in your Bible.

HOLD FAST WITHOUT WAVERING

"Let us hold fast the confession of our hope without wavering, for He who promised is faithful" (v. 23). Do you ever waver in your faith? I do.

Look at the positive and negative examples of "faith-wavering" in the margin. Why do we want to hold fast without wavering?

_____

And how are we to keep holding fast the confession of our hope without wavering? Notice the phrase "let us." We need to do it together. We can't do it on our own.

"Let us consider how to stimulate one another to love and good deeds" (v. 24). Have you ever blown on a fire when the coals were dying down? You blow all the embers off the coals and a new flame comes up. In the body of Christ, we are supposed to be doing that for each other. Sometimes sin or doubt or just the film of life itself puts a thick coating of soot on our lives, which makes it hard to connect with God. What we desperately need is for a loving brother or sister to come along and blow off the embers. We are supposed to be fanning the flames of love and good works in each other's lives. In the church, we stimulate each other to greater passion for God.

Every man needs brothers who are challenging him to be all he can be under God for his family. Every wife needs sisters in the Lord who are calling her to be a woman of virtue and a wife who makes her marriage stronger in the Lord. Do you have people like that in your life? The place to find them is at church.

Often I speak with believers who are wondering, "Why do I seem to be losing? Other people are racing ahead spiritually, but I'm just going along for a ride." It takes more than a weekend worship experience with God. It takes meaningful connectedness with the followers of Jesus Christ, believers getting together and challenging one another and exhorting one another. When that is happening for you on a regular basis, the blessings that flow into your family will be immense and immediate.

How has your church family stimulated you to love and serve God? _____

"He [Abraham] did not waver in unbelief at God's promise, but was strengthened in his faith and gave glory to God, because he was fully convinced that what He had promised He was also able to perform. Therefore, it was credited to him for righteousness" (Rom. 4:20-22, HCSB).

"Let him ask in faith, nothing wavering. For he that wavereth is like a wave of the sea driven with the wind and tossed. For let not that man think that he shall receive any thing of the Lord" (Jas. 1:6-7, KJV).

How have your stimulating relationships with God's people blessed your family?

_____

_____

Do Not Forsake But Encourage

"Not forsaking our own assembling together, as is the habit of some, but encouraging one another" (v. 25). The church isn't just about you getting what you need. It's about you participating in what everyone needs. It is a community of families all working together so the church can be all God wants it to be. When you pick up your responsibility to encourage others in the church, God will bless and prosper your own family.

I've found that 9 of every 10 people who are dissatisfied with their church are not participating. They are not worshiping regularly or fervently, they are not connected in meaningful relationships with others, and they have never rolled up their sleeves to get involved. If your church believes the Bible and teaches it, I guarantee you will get a lot more benefit for your family if you participate.

If you have been trying to go it alone, I urge you to get back to the church. It's where your family will grow and flourish in the Lord.

How is the Lord leading you to demonstrate to your family (and church family) your belief in, submission to, and participation in the local church?

_____

_____

To the Leader:

Before the Session

If you followed the "Before the Session" suggestion in Week 1, display the "Church" placard as well as the previous weeks' placards.

During the Session

1. Read Psalm 122:1. Ask: *Are you always glad when it's time to go to the house of the Lord? are your kids? Why is church important to you and your family?* OR Organize the class into two groups. Ask one group to describe what they would *like* their households to be like on Sunday mornings before church. Ask the other group to describe what their households are *really* like on most Sunday mornings before church. FOR EITHER OPTION Point out that the fact participants are in Sunday School means they value church. Today you will explore why *church* is a powerful word that can transform families.

2. Inquire: *According to 1 Timothy 3:15, why must we not let our families neglect the church?* Invite volunteers to share how God's church has supported their families when their lives were being shaken. Comment that some families can't say the church has been that helpful to them because they have not accessed the transforming benefits of the church. Ask what three things Dr. MacDonald said we must do to access the benefits of the church for our families (p. 55).

3. Ask a volunteer to read Matthew 16:13-18. Discuss the last activity of Day 1 (p. 56). Explain: *The fact that the church is built on the confession that Jesus is the Son of God is one reason we can believe in the church.*

4. Ask what *church* means. Discuss the first activity of Day 2 (p. 57). Ask what God does with us when He calls us out of this world. Read 1 Peter 2:4-5. Remark that we are living stones God is using to build His kingdom. Ask: *If you say you're into Jesus, why must you also be into the church? Why don't some Christians believe in the church? How can we love and believe in the church even if it has hurt us?* Explain that the church isn't all about us—it's all about Jesus! We can also believe in the church

Think about your relationship with your church staff. Are you a joy to lead? Find ways to remember and express appreciation to your church leaders this week—take them to lunch, write a note, give a hug and a thank you, and so forth.

when we realize that, in the end, we win. Discuss the third activity of Day 2 (p. 59). Ask: *What do you believe about the church of Jesus Christ?*

5. Read Hebrews 13:17. Discuss the first two activities of Day 3. Ask: *Does being responsible for your family feel heavy at times? Why? How many people are in your family? About how many people are in our church? Who is responsible for those souls?* Ask someone to read Hebrews 13:7. Ask: *What are we to do about our leaders who bear such heavy loads for our sake? What if we don't always agree with them?* Lead the class to come up with ways to remember your church staff in the coming year. Urge them to pray for your church staff daily. Remark that believers can also honor their church leaders by being a joy to lead. Examine what makes a person a joy to lead. Explore why a family can be transformed when the parents submit to church leaders and are faithful, available, and teachable.

6. Discuss the first activity of Day 4 (p. 61). Ask what role the church's weekly worship services play in helping believers draw near to God. Ask what four things Dr. MacDonald suggested to maximize the family's worship experience (p. 62). Suggest that at breakfast on Sunday morning (or supper on Saturday if Sunday mornings are too crazy) participants can prepare their families for worship by reading a portion of a Psalm. Psalm 92 would be a good place to start and read on from there each week.

7. Request that someone read Hebrews 10:23-25. Ask what else believers are to do since the barrier separating them from God has been removed. Discuss the second activity of Day 5 (p. 63). Explore how the church helps believers hold fast. Discuss the third activity. Ask what might cause families to forsake assembling with other believers. Point out that when storms come, sports and recreational activities aren't going to hold the family together—but God's church will. Discuss how the families represented in your class can participate in your church and encourage one another. Close in prayer. Invite participants to voice sentence prayers, using the prayer suggestions found at the conclusion of Day 3 (p. 61).

Commitment

Jesus on Commitment

GET OFF THE FENCE

At the center of an ever-successful family is a rock-solid commitment. An unswerving, unalterable, unending commitment to do life together under God. Let's study some teaching Jesus did on commitment and examine how He interacted with people who claimed to be committed—but were not.

Read Luke 14:25-26 in your Bible. Who was with Jesus and how were they demonstrating at least a surface commitment? _____

What did Jesus tell them constituted real commitment to Him? _____

_____

Anything less than total, 100 percent, radical commitment to Christ is not commitment at all.

You say, "What does He mean by hate my father and mother?" In Matthew 10:37, Jesus said it differently to His twelve disciples. As you read that verse in the margin, underline all the persons mentioned whom you love. Whom must you love above all those dear ones?

_____

"He who loves father or mother more than Me is not worthy of Me; and he who loves son or daughter more than Me is not worthy of Me" (Matt. 10:37).

67

That's what commitment is—to put Christ above everything.

As the parents of three wonderful children, Kathy and I have talked about the tension we feel with this truth. We love our kids so much that it is difficult at times not to feel we are in danger of loving them more than we love God. But to allow our kids to mean more to us than our relationship with the Lord is to put them in great danger. In fact, isn't that the whole point of God's actions toward Abraham and Isaac? God told Abraham, "You can't love anyone or anything more than Me, so get your son and take him up on the mountain and offer him on an altar there." You can check out Genesis 22 for the full story.

Your family also must come to grips with what it means for God to be your first and highest commitment. Anything less is not commitment at all. However, when God is in His rightful place, then that same kind of total commitment can flow to your family. Anything less than total commitment to Christ does not produce the power necessary to defeat your enemies, deliver your priorities, and destroy your obstacles. That's the kind of commitment God uses to bless our relationship with Him, and that's the kind of commitment God uses to make our family relationships all He desires them to be.

CALCULATE THE COST

You say, "That's pretty hard. Total commitment to my family will not come without a price." You're right, so make sure the cost of your commitment has been calculated. In Luke 14:27, Jesus declared, "Whoever does not carry his own cross and come after Me cannot be My disciple." The cross in this verse is symbolic of the hardships related to following Christ.

What are some of those hardships? _____

_____

For starters, life is a daily grind and every day you have to stay at it. Another cross we must pick up is the rejection that comes with following the Lord. Then there is the cross of having a new Master and living for Him, rather than for yourself. Remaining faithful to Christ, even through difficult circumstances, is a cross that every believer must carry.

Many other examples could be given to prove that picking up my cross and carrying it every day is not an easy life, but it is the only true Christian life. If I refuse to carry my cross daily, I cannot be Christ's disciple.

In Luke 14:28, Jesus gave an illustration: "Which one of you, when he wants to build a tower does not first sit down and calculate the cost to see if he has enough to complete it?" The word *calculate* was used in reference to a one-by-one count. That's the kind of measuring Jesus calls for when we are calculating what it will take to keep our commitments.

Can I finish the course? Can I be a faithful husband for my whole life? Can I be the wife God has called me to be? Am I willing to pay the price of godly parenting? If I am unwilling, I have no business making the commitment. Commitment is powerful when the cost is calculated.

day Two

Jesus on Commitment (Part 2)

A man I greatly respect said, "Commitment is the defining characteristic of a person's life." How true! There are people who keep their commitments, and there are people who don't. Do you keep the commitments you make?

FINISH THE COURSE

Read again about the tower in Luke 14:28-30. What happened when the builder didn't finish what he started?

_____

The word *ridicule* there means to mock or literally to play with a child. First John 2:19 says, "They went out from us, but they were not really of us; for if they had been of us, they would have remained with us; but they went out, so that it would be shown that they all are not of us." It is enduring to the end that proves the legitimacy of a profession of faith. Jesus Christ is very interested in us finishing what we start.

Commitment is a powerful tool for family transformation. Successful parenting is not simply getting your kids through high school or college. It grieves me so much when people say, "Just a couple more years and our kids will be grown and gone." What are they talking about? Parenting is a job for a hundred years!

You say, "I don't think I'm going to be around for a hundred years." No, but your children and your grandchildren will be. They'll know the kind of life you lived. They'll know the kind of opportunity you've given them. They'll know whether or not you were a person who kept your commitments.

What we do affects our children. It affects our grandchildren. Anybody can start something. The power of commitment is released into your family when you determine that under all circumstances, you will finish what you start.

> "The power of commitment is released into your family when you determine that under all circumstances, you will finish what you start."
> —James MacDonald

PAY THE PRICE

Perhaps you're thinking, *If commitment is such a great thing, why don't more people have it?* That's a great question, and the answer is seen in Jesus' final illustration on commitment from Luke 14:31: "What king, when he sets out to meet another king in battle, will not first sit down and consider whether he is strong enough with ten thousand men to encounter the one coming against him with twenty thousand?"

The king asks, "How many do we have?" "Are we stronger?" And he begins to count the cost and determine if he is willing to pay the price. "Can we win? How many casualties will there be? Are we willing to live with the consequences of what we are committing to?"

"While the other is still far away, he sends a delegation and asks for terms of peace" (v. 32). If you can't win, stay out of the battle. Kings who defend their kingdoms only until hardship comes or suffering is required or a price must be paid don't have their kingdoms very long. Similarly, people who follow Christ only until someone rejects them for their faith or their integrity costs them their job or they become weary of the pursuit of holiness don't follow Christ very long. Families that stay together and keep growing only until difficulties come or conflicts arise or a price must be paid never become all God would have them be and never experience the joy of successful family living.

Absolute, total commitment. Even when a price has to be paid.

What price do you need to be paying to demonstrate total commitment to your family?

❑ **My career**   ❑ **My desires**

❑ **My rest**   ❑ **My child's happiness with me**

❑ **Other:** _____

day Three

Why Do Families Break Their Commitments?

Why is it so hard to be committed? Why do families break their commitments? Why do husbands and wives walk out on each other? Why do children disown their parents and vice versa? Here are three reasons taken from Luke 9. I think you'll recognize them.

REASON #1: COST NOT COUNTED AHEAD OF TIME

"As they were going along the road, someone said to Him, 'I will follow you wherever You go' " (9:57). That sounds pretty good, doesn't it? On one level, you have to respect the guy. After all, he has his job right: "I am going to be following. I don't have any maps. I don't have any plans. I don't have any ideas. I don't have any agendas. I am going to be on Your program, Lord." He also has the roles right: "You're the boss; I am the employee. I am going to be the follower; You are going to be the leader." And then he has the extent right: "I will follow You wherever You go—hills, valleys, cities, countries, highs, lows, good times, bad times." If a guy like that shows up at the average church, they're like, "Sign him up!" And he will be up giving his testimony in three weeks.

But notice Jesus' response in verse 58: "The foxes have holes and the birds of the air have nests, but the Son of Man has nowhere to lay His head." He was saying, "Dude, you don't know what you're talking about. You haven't counted the cost. Are you going to follow Me wherever I go? Do you know where I go? Do you know I don't even have a place to sleep at night?" The man had expressed such a strong desire to be committed, but he had not counted the cost. And Christ rejected him.

Look up the following passages. Record phrases from each verse that describe the cost-counting commitment to your family that Christ will not reject.

Galatians 6:2 _____

2 Timothy 2:10 _____

1 Peter 4:19 _____

Maybe you are at a place where your commitment to your family is costing you a lot. Maybe your marriage is taking a lot more energy than it has at other times. Maybe you are carrying a heavy burden for one of your children, and you are wondering if keeping your commitment is really worth all it is costing you. Don't give up! The power that comes on the other side of commitment is incredible, but the pain of breaking your family commitments is something from which few people ever recover.

None of us knows what is around the corner. You may have something very difficult drop out of nowhere and severely test your family's commitment. Don't give up. Keep pressing on one day at a time, or if need be, one step at a time.

Read Colossians 1:28-29 in the margin. Where can you

find the strength to keep pressing on?_____

_____

It's when you want most to throw in the towel that you must press in and push forward, drawing upon the Lord's strength to keep the commitments you have made to your family.

There is power in that! The families that you respect, the ones you see doing so well—they have this; I guarantee it. And you can have it too. But there is a cost that must be counted ahead of time.

"We proclaim him, admonishing and teaching everyone with all wisdom, so that we may present everyone perfect in Christ. To this end I labor, struggling with all his energy, which so powerfully works in me" (Col. 1:28-29, NIV).

Why Do Families Break Their Commitments? (Part 2)

REASON #2: PRICE NOT PAID DURING HARDSHIP

Look at Luke 9:59-60. This time the invitation comes from Jesus: "He said to another, 'Follow Me.' But he [answered], 'Lord, permit me first to go and bury my father.' But He said to him, 'Allow the dead to bury their own dead; but as for you, go and proclaim everywhere the kingdom of God.' " That seems like a reasonable request: "Let me go bury my father, and then I am with You." For Jewish people, the burial of a family member was the supreme duty. Rabbis were permitted to be absent at worship even on holy days to bury a family member. However, Christ is not questioning the reasonableness of his request.

The reason Jesus rejects this man as a committed disciple is because of his first four words: "Lord, permit me first." "Lord, me first" just doesn't work. Even the greatest of human obligations must not compete with allegiance to Christ. In a similar way, no human activity or responsibility should interfere with my family: not work, not leisure, not friends, not education.

That's a high price, but the failure to pay the price will bring devastation to your family. It's not always easy to be a father. It's not always easy to be a mother. It's not always easy to be a faithful spouse. But the price must be paid, even during hardship. If not, the commitment will break down.

Read Philippians 2:3-5 in your Bible. What price must you pay to demonstrate commitment to your family?

_____

_____

Who are you imitating when you don't say, "me first"?

_____

_____

REASON #3: COURSE NOT FINISHED

"Another also said, 'I will follow You, Lord; but first permit me to say good-bye to those at home.' But Jesus said to him, 'No one, after putting his hand to the plow and looking back, is fit for the kingdom of God' " (Luke 9:61-62). That is commitment in God's kingdom. Keep your hand on the plow. We are not looking back. This is what we committed ourselves to do, and we are going to keep on doing it for the rest of our lives.

Maybe the big issue for you is not divorce or estrangement or abandonment. Perhaps the issue at your house is that you fly off the handle, and you never apologize or make things right. Maybe you don't know how to say you're sorry. Perhaps you are so consumed with work or distracted by other things that you don't focus on your son or daughter. Maybe you neglect your marriage and don't give your spouse the emotional nourishment he or she longs for. You signed up for life. Finish the course!

"I have fought the good fight, I have finished the course, I have kept the faith" (2 Tim. 4:7).

Read 2 Timothy 4:7 in the margin. What's making you feel like giving up (even a little) on your family? List those things in the margin.

How will you demonstrate your commitment to finish the course? _____

_____

How Can I Sharpen My Family Commitment?

Here are four words to help you improve the commitment in your family.

CONSECRATE

The word *consecrate* means to declare holy or to set apart for the worship of God. Repent of a halfhearted, shallow commitment to your family.

Repent of selfishness and distractedness and avoidance of your number one responsibility under God—your family. Go to some of your family members and ask for forgiveness. Be specific. Say, "I'm sorry. I haven't been the mother God wants me to be. I have been distracted by other things." Or, "I haven't been the husband God wants me to be. Please forgive me."

Don't be ashamed to acknowledge before your family that God is dealing with your heart. Things can be different. God wants them to be different. It can start with you.

Read 2 Corinthians 8:5 in the margin. The proper order for consecration in the family is to set yourself apart

first _____ and then _____.

"They did not do as we expected, but they gave themselves first to the Lord and then to us in keeping with God's will" (2 Cor. 8:5, NIV).

COMMUNICATE

Gather your family together and say, "Hey, we are the _____ (fill in your family name). We keep our commitments." Give your family a vision of absolute, total commitment. Say to each other: "Absolute, total commitment. That's what we're all about. You don't ever have to worry if Mom and Dad are going to be around. We are going to be around! You don't ever have to worry if you hear us fighting that we are not going to work it out because we are going to work it out! We are in this for life!"

Speak that vision over your family, and watch the transforming power of God begin to build in your home.

What are some commitments your family members

need to keep?_____

_____

How can you communicate that to them?

_____

_____

COOPERATE

A big part of commitment is give and take. I can't always have my way. I can't do everything I want to do—not if I want to have the family of my dreams. I can't have my cake and eat it too. Sometimes I have to give in.

"OK, I'll stay home tonight. You go out." "Yeah, I'll come home a little bit early." "OK, I won't do that on Saturday. We need to do some family things. No problem. This comes first."

CHRIST

Christ is vital in the process of sharpening your family's commitment. This is definitely one of those "don't-try-this-at-home" messages. If you think this is some sort of pep talk on commitment, it isn't. You do not have within yourself the strength to do what I am talking about doing. If it doesn't emerge from a personal intimacy with Christ, if it doesn't emerge from a complete surrender under His lordship, it will never happen.

Maybe in this moment you are thinking, *O God, I am not proud of everything that has been. I am not proud of everything that I have said and done.* But here is the marvelous news of the grace of God. It matters not what has been; what matters is what can be. By God's grace you can be a person of commitment.

> "It matters not what has been; what matters is what can be. By God's grace you can be a person of commitment."
> —James MacDonald

Read Joshua 24:14-15 in your Bible and list what makes a successful, happy, God-honoring family.

_____

_____

What is your commitment today?

As for me and my house, _____

_____ .

Communicate that commitment to your family.

To the Leader:

Contact your class members this week and thank them for their commitment to this study. Recommit yourself to be the teacher God desires through ample study and preparation for each class session.

Before the Session

If you followed the "Before the Session" suggestion in Week 1, display the "Commitment" placard as well as the previous weeks' placards.

During the Session

1. Ask: *What are words of commitment spoken in families? Can you remember your marriage vows? Did you make a formal commitment to your children? How? Why do we make formal commitments? Today we will discuss the necessity of making and, more importantly, keeping commitments.* OR Ask participants what unfinished projects they have lying around at home. Inquire: *Why is it often difficult to finish what we start?* Share that unfinished needlework or woodwork might not be that big a deal, but if our families are going to be transformed, we must be totally committed to finish what we start with our spouse and children.

2. Discuss the questions related to Luke 14:25-26 in Day 1 (p. 67). Ask: *How are a lot of families like that crowd? What's the difference between traveling with Jesus and being totally committed to Him?* Use Matthew 10:37 to explore what Jesus meant by "hate your father." Ask: *How can absolute commitment to Christ transform our families—wouldn't it tear them down instead? Explain.* Summarize the events of Genesis 22:1-11. Ask participants to read Genesis 22:12 and share what God wants to know about every believer. Ask someone to read Genesis 22:15-18. Inquire: *What will God do for you and your family if you put Him above all? How might it actually give our children a sense of security to know God comes before them in our lives?*

3. Explain: *Once we nail down that our top priority is Christ, we must determine our next full commitment is to our families. All the passages we will look at this week seem to imply that we must ignore our families and focus on God. However, based on 1 Timothy 5:8 we know that's not true.* (Read that verse aloud.) Inform participants you will take the principles Jesus taught about commitment to Him and apply them to making a total commitment to your families. A total commitment to Christ will lead to

a total commitment to family. Encourage participants to keep that dual purpose in mind as you study.

4. Discuss the first activity of Day 2 (p. 69). Ask: *How will we, and consequently Christ, be ridiculed if we don't finish the course with Christ and our families?* Ask someone to read the quotation in the margin of Day 2 (p. 70). Explore how that kind of commitment can transform a marriage and children. Ask a volunteer to read Luke 14:31-33. Discuss: *What are the costs of being fully committed to family? Why are those costs worth it?*

5. Ask the questions posed by Dr. MacDonald at the beginning of Day 3. Read Luke 9:57-58. Ask why Jesus rejected the man's statement of commitment. Discuss the first activity of Day 3 (p. 72). Explain that Galatians 2:20 sums up what it means to be totally committed to Christ. Read that verse. Point out: *When you've died with Christ, you're willing to carry those family burdens, endure anything for their sake, and continue to do them good even when times are tough.* Discuss the second activity of Day 3. Ask: *What should be our goal for our families according to Colossians 1:28? What words from verse 29 tell you it's not going to be easy? What words assure you that you can do it?*

6. Request that someone read Luke 9:59-60. Ask what words in the man's request give insight into his real reason for not following Jesus. Ask how "me first" gets in the way of family commitment. Discuss the first activity of Day 4 (p. 73). Ask what will happen if this price of humbly putting others first isn't paid. Read Luke 9:61-62. Explore other ways parents fail to finish the course besides divorce or abandonment. Ask someone to read 2 Timothy 4:7. Discuss ways believers must fight for their marriages (instead of with their marriage partner!) and finish the course with their children.

7. Ask the class to share and describe the four ways Dr. MacDonald said believers can sharpen their family commitment (pp. 74-76). Discuss the first activity of Day 5. Ask why the order of consecration stated in 2 Corinthians 8:5 is important. Discuss the final activity of Day 5. Urge participants to make their own family commitment to serve the Lord. Close in prayer.

Love

What the Bible Says About Love

Our final word is the very air that transformed families breathe. It is the soil in which the previous six words can germinate and grow. Without love, our pursuit of transformation will grate on our families and cause strife. With love, our energies can soothe, even when the road to change is not smooth.

Scripture has much to say about the transforming power of love and about what it can do for a broken marriage, a severed relationship, or a struggling family. The Scriptures tell us:

• *Love is a family debt worth having*: "Owe nothing to anyone except to love one another" (Rom. 13:8).

• *Love keeps our families thinking clearly*: "If we are of sound mind, it is … the love of Christ [that] controls us" (2 Cor. 5:13-14).

• *Love fuels family harmony*: " Walk … with all humility and gentleness, with patience, showing tolerance for one another in love" (Eph. 4:1-2).

• *Love binds our families together*: "Their hearts … [have] been knit together in love" (Col. 2:2).

• *Love keeps us from focusing on family failures*: "Keep fervent in your love for one another, because love covers a multitude of sins" (1 Pet. 4:8).

• *God's love allows us to conquer every family obstacle*: "In all these things we overwhelmingly conquer through Him who loved us" (Rom. 8:37).

Many people don't consider love as they think about fixing and adjusting and growing and changing their families. First Corinthians 13 highlights five things people think can do more to change their families than love.

"Faith, hope, love, abide these three; but the greatest of these is love" (1 Cor. 13:13).

Read 1 Corinthians 13:1-3 in your Bible and complete this statement: Anything I do in, with, or for my family

without love is _____

1. *Talk.* "If I speak with the tongues of men and of angels, but do not have love, I have become a noisy gong or a clanging cymbal" (v. 1). A lot of people think talk will change their family. "We are going to sit down and have a talk. I know some things that you don't, and you're going to hear them right now." I am all for families talking things through, but if your words are not backed up by love, it doesn't matter how eloquent you are or how clear you make things. Communication that is not rooted in love is not only fruitless; but it is also counterproductive to the things God wants to do in your family.

2. *Knowledge.* "If I have the gift of prophecy, and know all mysteries and all knowledge" (v. 2). Send your child to a good school. Encourage him to get good grades and earn a scholarship to a major university. We can train our children to think like Einstein and write like a Pulitzer prize winning author, but without love it amounts to nothing.

3. *Faith.* Some people think faith can do more than love for their family. "If I have all faith, so as to remove mountains" (v. 2). That is big-time faith! Hebrews 11:6 teaches that it is impossible to please God without faith. But you can have all the faith in the world, and if you don't have love, you have a big bag of zilch. Faith can't exist by itself; it has to be rooted in love.

4. *Compassion.* "If I give all my possessions to feed the poor ... but do not have love, it profits me nothing" (v. 3). Not feeding the poor, not supporting single parents, not even sending dollars to Africa will have an impact on your family if there is a lack of love at home. Compassion alone will not change your family.

5. *Sacrifice.* "If I surrender my body to be burned, but do not have love, it profits me nothing" (v. 3). If I were to literally give up my life for my family, but I didn't love them or they didn't know that I loved them, it would be worthless.

What sacrifices do you make for your family?

_____

_____

What's your most common attitude when sacrificing for your family?

❑ **Resentment**
❑ **Resigned martyrdom**
❑ **Love**
❑ **Other:** _____

Love Protects

Read 1 Corinthians 13:8 in the margin. How powerful

is love? _____

Love never fails to win back the heart of a distant loved one who has grown cold and hard. Love never fails to conquer years of neglect. Love never fails to bring a stubborn, willful child back into the fold.

As you read 1 Corinthians 13:7 in the margin, circle what love always does.

Love protects. "This is the message which you have heard from the beginning, that we should love one another" (1 John 3:11). This message is not a new one. It's the same stuff Jesus told His disciples in John 13:34-35: "A new commandment I give to you, that you love one another, even as I have loved you. … By this all men will know that you are My disciples, if you have love for one another."

Biblical love is protecting love. John gives a graphic illustration of what happens when we abandon protecting love: "We should love one another; not as Cain, who was of the evil one and slew his brother" (1 John 3:11-12). Cain was the son of Adam and Eve—the firstborn son who brutally murdered his younger brother.

Why would he do something like that? Why would a person kill a member of his family? People do it both literally and figuratively all the time. While it's only the literal murders you hear about in the papers, people all around us are dying in their families!

"Love never fails; but if there are gifts of prophecy, they will be done away; if there are tongues, they will cease; if there is knowledge, it will be done away" (1 Cor. 13:8).

"It always protects, always trusts, always hopes, always perseveres" (1 Cor. 13:7, NIV).

As a pastor, I regularly hear stories about families who are divided and fighting over the estate of their parents. And then there are the children who are tearing their families apart through rebellion. Why do people do stuff like that? "For what reason did [Cain] slay him? Because his deeds were evil, and his brother's were righteous" (1 John 3:12). Never underestimate the conflict that rages in the heart of a person who is in the process of rejecting God. Never underestimate the tension that person feels between your life and theirs.

The text gives not only the reason a person would do such things—"because his deeds were evil, and his brother's were righteous" and because "men loved the darkness rather than the Light" (John 3:19)—but also the source of this evil, this conflict: "Not as Cain, who was of the evil one." All evil in our world is rooted ultimately in the father of evil, Satan. Satan, the one who shattered the first family in history through his influence over Cain, has the same goal today: to shatter your family.

"Your adversary, the devil, prowls around like a roaring lion, seeking someone to devour" (1 Pet. 5:8). Some people, through their own disobedience and failure to rely upon God, are vulnerable to being devoured. Satan wants to devour your marriage. Satan wants to devour your children. He wants to have them, and he wants the world to have them. He wants to bring reproach on the name of Christ. That's the battle in which each of us is engaged.

The way we think to stop Satan in his tracks is not God's way to do so. Our approach is to draw the line and stand our ground. Raise our fists and stick up for our rights. The biblical way, the way to cooperate with what God is doing in this world, is the way of love. That is our protection.

Read Luke 6:27-31. What is the way of love?

_____

Read Luke 6:35. What results from following the way

of love?_____

Genesis 4 tells us that God put a mark on Cain, and he went his own way and wandered in the wilderness the rest of his life. The way of Cain is opposite the way of love. People who take the way of Cain—the way of hatred instead of love—still wander in a wilderness and miss the good things of life that God desires to give them. When we love in return for hate, when we turn the other cheek, when we go the second mile, we avoid the life of Cain. We choose the way of love, and we experience God's protection and covering over our families.

Love Is Proof

Read 1 John 3:13-14 in the margin and underline what you prove when you live God's way of love.

> "Do not be surprised, brethren, if the world hates you. We know that we have passed out of death into life, because we love the brethren" (1 John 3:13-14).

Who are the "brethren"? They are our brothers and sisters in Christ at church and at home. They are people to whom we have made a long-term commitment—to love them through thick and thin, through ups and downs, and to keep on going together through life. People who make those kinds of commitments are proving something.

The love talked about in 1 John 3:14 conveys continuous action, continual loving. Jesus said in Luke 6:32 that if you only love people who love you—what's the big deal about that? Even sinners do that! The big deal is if you can love people who hate you, if you can love people who use you, if you can love people who neglect you. That proves something! It proves you have truly grasped the magnitude of Christ's love for you, and that you have passed from death to life.

HATRED IS MURDER

"Everyone who hates his brother is a murderer; and you know that no murderer has eternal life abiding in him" (1 John 3:15). Why is hatred the same as murder? Because God looks at your heart, not just at your actions. God says, "It's just the same to Me as if you did kill them. I am not looking at what you do; I don't have to. I am looking at who you are and what you feel." If your heart is filled with hatred, you are a murderer. And no murderer has eternal life.

So here's the question. Do you truly know Jesus? Have you really turned from your sin and embraced Christ for your forgiveness? Do you have a personal relationship with Him? If you do, then you don't hate people.

You say, "People have hurt me." People have hurt me too, and I have had to labor on my knees to get to a good place with them. That's where you need to be; it's the place of living according to love.

Read 1 John 4:19-21 and answer the following:

What does God call people who claim love for Him but

hate others? _____

How can you possibly love people who have hurt you?

_____

_____

IS YOUR LOVE GROWING?

Unquenchable, unconquerable, unstoppable love is proof you really know the Savior. "We know love by this, that He laid down His life for us; and we ought to lay down our lives for the brethren" (1 John 3:16). If you truly know Christ, there will be a growing pattern of love in your life.

Are you growing in your capacity to love?

Check the following statements that are true of you.

❑ 1. *I love more people than ever before.* How many people do you love? Has the number increased since you became a follower of Jesus Christ? That's what the Christian life is all about. If you are plugged into the Master, then you are growing in your capacity to love. And that means loving more people than ever before.

❑ 2. *I love more kinds of people than ever before.* I pray often that the racial and cultural diversity of our church will exceed that of our surrounding community. We want to be known as a place where people are loved, not as a place where people are looked at and measured and assessed according to externals that don't matter to God. That's the world, not the kingdom of Christ. How are you doing in this? Are you growing in your capacity to love more kinds of people than ever before?

❑ 3. *I love over longer periods of time than ever before.* What could be better than looking into the face of a person whom you have loved for many years and saying, "I am still loving you, brother! You are still loving me. We are in this together."

Read 1 Thessalonians 3:12 in the margin. Voice this verse as a personal prayer, asking God to increase your love for your family, church family, and all people.

"May the Lord make your love increase and overflow for each other and for everyone else, just as ours does for you" (1 Thess. 3:12, NIV).

day Four

Love at Home

Love is proof. And this kind of love is urgently needed in our marriages and with our children. Here's why: You can change your job—people do it all the time. If your neighbors are driving you nuts, you can always move across town. And you can even change churches. But you cannot change your family.

If ever there were a place where you needed a growing capacity for love, it's in the home. Stick it out. Persevere in love. Prove with your life that you really do know Jesus Christ. Don't give up.

Go back and humble yourself and say you're sorry. Start again. Get on your knees and pray for the love of Christ to permeate your marriage, your home, every relationship you have.

Read John 13:1 in the margin. What does it mean to you to love a family member "to the end"?

"Before the Feast of the Passover, Jesus knowing that His hour had come that He would depart out of this world to the Father, having loved His own who were in the world, He loved them to the end" (John 13:1).

_____

_____

LOVE IS PRACTICAL

"Whoever has the world's goods, and sees his brother in need and closes his heart against him, how does the love of God abide in him?" (1 John 3:17). Can you picture the scenario described here? Suppose you see a homeless man lying by the side of the street. He tries like anything to make eye contact with you. He says something like, "Can you help me? Do you have any money? Would you assist me?" You might be tempted to close your heart toward him: *If I give him some money, he will just drink it away. How can I be sure he is not a con artist? Most likely he has already rejected the help of his own family. Why should I help him?* These are the mental gymnastics of closing your heart to love.

Several years ago the Lord dealt very strongly with me about this very thing. I have made a commitment to Him since that time, that, if I have anything in my wallet and I see a person in need, I will never refuse to help him or her. I have a lot of loving to do in this life, and I can't afford to close my heart when God is working to open it wider and wider. I must always be seeking to expand my capacity to love in practical ways.

"Little children, let us not love with word or with tongue, but in deed and truth" (v. 18). I don't mean to imply that love is only about helping people in that kind of acute need. My point is this: Your heart is either opening or closing to this concept of love. Don't think you can fool God—He knows the truth.

If your heart is opening up to love, you will see every opportunity in your life as a chance to "love [not just] with word or with tongue, but in deed and truth."

> "Giving up something I value to enrich the life of someone else—that's love."
> — James MacDonald

Giving up something I value to enrich the life of someone else—that's love. But many people don't get this "enriching the life of another" stuff. They say, "I'll do these things for you, if you do these things for me." That's the typical marriage. The problem is when the husband stops doing his part, the wife stops doing hers. There is nothing loving about that. That is merely a contractual relationship. Love says, "I am not counting what you're doing. I am not measuring and I am not keeping score. I am trying to enrich your life; I am spending myself so that your life can be better."

I must be concerned about what you need. Whether you are or are not concerned about what I need is a secondary matter. Love keeps on acting, keeps on waiting, keeps on working, and keeps on trusting God to produce the needed changes in others.

Record the names of your family members below. Next to each name, state one way you will demonstrate unselfish, active love to that person this week.

_____

_____

_____

_____

Love Is Priority

"We will know by this that we are of the truth, and will assure our heart before Him in whatever our heart condemns us" (1 John 3:19-20). Does your heart ever condemn you? It's not the Holy Spirit condemning you; it's a weak, uninformed conscience.

Read 1 John 3:18-20 in your Bible and fill in the blank. When your conscience is accusing you, you will know

by _____ that you are of the truth.

A lifestyle of love will give us the assurance we need. So the next time your heart starts condemning you, you can respond, "I am not what I could be, and I am not what I should be, but praise the Lord I am not what I was. I am a daughter of God. I am a son of the Father. I have a growing capacity to love. It doesn't matter what you say about me. God has set His love upon me. I am in process, and I am moving forward."

If that doesn't put an end to the condemnation, then notice the last part of verse 20: "God is greater than our heart and knows all things." At

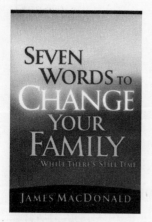

the end of the day, it doesn't really matter what I say about myself. What matters is what God says about me and what His Word says about me. That's why it is important for us to study God's Word regularly—so we can know what it means to follow Christ and grow in Him. We don't have to have a weak, uninformed conscience that condemns us; we can have a growing understanding of the truth. So the next time you find yourself wondering, "Am I really a Christian?" just ask yourself this question, "Am I growing in love?"

"Beloved, if our heart does not condemn us, we have confidence before God; and whatever we ask we receive from Him, because we keep His commandments and do the things that are pleasing in His sight" (1 John 3:21-22). This Christian life thing really works. And it all starts with love. Love leads to confidence; confidence leads to prayer; prayer leads to answers; answers to more obedience. Love fuels the whole thing.

LOVE IS PRIORITY NUMBER ONE

Consider for a moment everything we've studied together. All of it flows from love. How could you possibly forgive someone unless you love him or her? Why would you bless your children or honor your parents apart from love? Truth is love's greatest ally. The local church is the place where you practice love to others. And commitments are kept only because of love.

Only when we recognize we don't have this kind of love can we begin to understand that it comes only from a relationship with Christ. It is the cross of Christ, the perfect example of love, that enables us to live a life of love. "This is His commandment, that we believe in the name of His Son Jesus Christ, and love one another, just as He commanded us" (1 John 3:23). Go after this love for yourself and for your family. It will transform you.

Think back over those seven powerful words we have been studying. Which are the most difficult for you to implement in your life and family? (Circle all that apply.)

Forgiveness	**Blessing**
Honor	**Truth**
Church	**Commitment**
Love	

Read Romans 13:8-10 in the margin. Why would a wholehearted commitment to love your family take care of the other six words?

_____

_____

"Owe nothing to anyone except to love one another; for he who loves his neighbor has fulfilled the law. For this, "YOU SHALL NOT COMMIT ADULTERY, YOU SHALL NOT MURDER, YOU SHALL NOT STEAL, YOU SHALL NOT COVET," and if there is any other commandment, it is summed up in this saying, "YOU SHALL LOVE YOUR NEIGHBOR AS YOURSELF." Love does no wrong to a neighbor; therefore love is the fulfillment of the law" (Rom. 13:8-10).

NOTES

To the Leader:

Adults in your class may be interested in studying the newly revised *The Five Love Languages* by Dr. Gary Chapman. Check your local LifeWay Christian Store or *www.lifeway.com.* for more information.

Before the Session

1. If you followed the "Before the Session" suggestion in Week 1, display the "Love" placard as well as the previous weeks' placards.
2. Prepare a large writing surface (board, poster, etc.) for use during the session.

During the Session

1. Ask: *As you think back over the seven words we've studied, why do you think Dr. MacDonald said, "Without love, our pursuit of transformation will grate on our families and cause strife"? Why do we need to study love? Can't we just try harder to love more?* OR Ask participants what accessory they absolutely must have on before they feel completely dressed. Comment that we've got to have those belts (men) and earrings (ladies) to pull our outfits together. Read Colossians 3:12-14. Ask what a believer absolutely must put on to bind together all the other Christian virtues. Point out that love also binds together all the transformational words you've studied the past six weeks. Ask someone to read the first paragraph of Day 1 (p. 79). FOR EITHER OPTION Explain that the world defines *love* many ways. In order to be transformed, families need to learn and display "God's Way of Love" (write that over a column on the board).

2. Request that participants refer to Day 1 and share what God's love will do in families. Invite someone to read 1 Corinthians 13:1-3. Encourage volunteers to share how they completed the statement in the first activity of Day 1 (p. 79). Ask what people often use in attempts to improve their families. Explore why those aren't any good without love. Explore how parents can sacrifice for their families and their families still not know they love them.

3. Ask someone to read 1 Corinthians 13:4-7. Direct the class to share what love is and is not. Write responses to what love is under "God's Way of Love" on the board. Discuss the first activity of Day 2 (p. 81). Ask someone to read the first paragraph of Day 2. Ask: *Do we really believe*

that? Invite volunteers to share how they have personally observed that love never fails.

4. Explain that love never fails to protect us. Ask someone to read 1 John 3:11-12. Ask: *Why would John use the illustration of Cain when there are many examples of hate in Scripture?* Remark that it is particularly heinous to kill your own brother. Explore how family members figuratively kill one another today. Write "Way of Cain" over a second column on the board. Request that participants read Genesis 4:3-12 and identify why Cain acted as he did. Write responses on the board. Ask what results from following Cain's way. Read 1 Peter 5:8-9. Ask: *How can we resist Satan and avoid following the way of Cain?* [Follow God's way of love.] Record participants' responses to the last activity of Day 2 (p. 82) under "God's Way of Love." Ask participants to silently compare the two columns on the board and determine which best describes them.

5. Discuss the first two activities of Day 3. Ask the class to share and explain the three ways Dr. MacDonald said we can know we are growing in love (pp. 84-85).

6. Ask: *What impact can growing in love for all people have on our family relationships? Why is it often most difficult to demonstrate God's way of love at home?* Discuss the first activity of Day 4. Request that someone read the definition of love in the margin of Day 4 (p. 85). Ask if participants think "I give 50 percent, you give 50 percent" is a good working percentage for a family and why. Read 1 John 3:16. Ask what percentage Jesus gave. Ask: *What valued things might we need to give up to enrich the lives of our family members? What if they don't give anything back?* Encourage participants to act on the final activity of Day 4.

7. Discuss the first activity of Day 5 (p. 87). Ask how our hearts condemn us, especially at home. Ask: *Why does the truth that God is greater than your heart and knows all things comfort you?* Ask someone to read 1 John 3:21-22. Share that when we walk in God's way of love our hearts don't condemn us. Discuss: *What do we have when our hearts don't condemn us? What does confidence lead us to do? What will occur when we pray? What will answered prayer lead to? How does this progression prove that love is the very fuel that energizes family strength and transformation?* Discuss the last question of Day 5. Read aloud 1 Peter 4:8 and close in prayer.

O. S. Hawkins

is President and Chief Executive Officer of GuideStone Financial Resources, formerly the Annuity Board of the Southern Baptist Convention. Previously he was pastor of First Baptist Church of Dallas (1993-1997) and of First Baptist Church of Fort Lauderdale, FL (1978-1993). He holds graduate degrees from Southwestern Baptist Theological Seminary and Luther Rice Seminary. He has been married to his wife Susie since 1970. They have two grown daughters. He is the author of more than 20 books.

JOE BECKLER wrote the personal learning activities and teaching plans for this study. Joe holds a Master of Divinity degree from New Orleans Baptist Theological Seminary. Currently he is planting a church in Durango, Colorado. He enjoys participating in outdoor sports. Joe and Cheri also parent triplet sons. Joe is an experienced curriculum writer for LifeWay.

ABOUT THIS STUDY

Briefly describe a situation where you felt helpless.

_____

_____

Based on your own experience, as well as your observation of others, identify two to three "moral earthquakes" that have created a sense of helplessness.

_____

_____

Moral Earthquakes and Secret Faults

Earthquakes can be utterly terrifying. When the earth trembles and jolts beneath our feet, not only are we disoriented and thrown into panic but the structures with which we surround ourselves crumble and topple. What only moments before provided our greatest comfort and security is suddenly transformed into a hostile environment of hurtling possessions and collapsing walls. The fright is almost beyond comprehension.

When a quake strikes, we are helpless in the face of gargantuan forces of destruction. But, as devastating as geological earthquakes are, moral earthquakes can be even more terrifying. While geographical disturbances are relatively few and far between, it seems that moral disruptions abound.

Our culture is in dire straits, reeling from the effects of societal seismic shifts, precisely because so many of us—men, women, and children—suffer from moral earthquakes ourselves. We have too easily succumbed to powerful temptations that ultimately topple our sure expectations and best intentions. Often hidden beneath the surface of our lives—like the secret faults beneath the crust of the earth—these temptations seem all but irresistible.

But there is hope. That is what these lessons are all about. They don't offer a quick fix. There is no magic wand, but as Christians we need not remain at the mercy of the hidden fault lines in our lives. Even in the aftermath of terrible moral disruption, we need not simply "let nature take its course." The Bible gives us a positive and practical agenda of protection and restoration that we can—and indeed, we must—follow.

O. S. Hawkins

Living on the Fault Line

day One

Geological and Moral Fault Lines

Earthquakes don't just happen. They are caused by things beyond our sight, well beneath the surface of the ground. The seams between the earth's various plates are called "faults." Usually, pressure along the fault line remains fairly subtle and stable. But over time, stress builds between the plates. When the tension finally exceeds the breaking strength of rock, a jolting rupture ensues. The earth is literally sundered, and the result can be utterly devastating. Earthquakes, however, are preceded by a series of smaller seismic events along the fault line—events beyond our sight that may have been quietly occurring beneath the surface for many years.

Not surprisingly, moral earthquakes follow the same pattern. They don't just happen.

We all know men and women whose actions have resulted in what we might call a moral earthquake: prominent pastors who fall into gross immorality, successful businessmen who are caught in illegal dealings, or happy families suddenly destroyed by unforeseen forces. We look at such people and wonder, *How could this have possibly happened?* Stunned and amazed, we say, "They looked like they were the all-American family." Or, "He seemed as if he really had it all together." Or, "She was so wonderful." Bewildered, we ask, "How can this be? They appeared to have everything going for them. What could have caused this terrible catastrophe to happen?"

Like geological earthquakes, moral earthquakes are preceded by the pressures of long-hidden faults. They erupt when the ordinary pressures of life finally expose the secret cracks in the character of a man or a woman or a family. Inevitably, the pressures of life expose the cracks in our characters. They reveal the secret faults that run beneath the surface of our lives. One day they erupt into a moral earthquake that has devastating results upon all those around us.

Describe a character-affecting "secret crack" that can precede a large moral downfall.

_____

What devastating effects do moral earthquakes create in people's lives?

_____

FROM HERO TO ZERO

Samson is a striking biblical example of a man who suffered a horrendous moral earthquake. His all-too-familiar story is told in the Book of Judges. He was a man who had it all going for him. He was young, strong, attractive, and influential—a natural leader. He came from a good family and enjoyed all the advantages of a solid moral upbringing. Yet in the end, his life was ruined by a moral earthquake.

Of course, it didn't just happen. In fact, Samson's moral earthquake was preceded by years of little faults—faults that began so insignificantly that we might be tempted to believe there was hardly anything to them. In fact, they ran their course over a period of two decades, cracking his character beneath the surface until a catastrophic earthquake became inevitable.

So what was it that really caused Samson's failure? What was his secret fault? Many of us who have a cursory acquaintance with his story might be tempted to blurt out, "Delilah."

We tend to make a big deal about Delilah. But in reality, some twenty years before that, a few little secret faults began to run their course through the character of Samson's life, cracking it here and there, finally resulting in a catastrophic moral collapse. Delilah just happened to be there at the end.

List two to three words that come to mind when you hear Samson's name.

_____

_____

day Two

A Terrible Demise

Samson's story is one of the saddest in the Bible—because he began so well, only to squander every advantage and every opportunity.

Read Judges 13:1-5 printed in the margin.

The story of Samson is set against the backdrop of the time of the judges. Once again the people of Israel found themselves under the fierce tyranny of the Philistines. Samson's birth was an answer to the fervent prayers of his godly parents. In addition, an angel of the Lord announced that Samson would one day be a champion to deliver his people from their despicable bondage.

Notice the great advantages that Samson had. He was dedicated from birth. He was a true gift of God to a sweet, godly couple. He was given a special calling. Indeed, he proved to be strong, clever, and winsome—the sort of young man destined for success in life. Nevertheless, though he started out on a godly track, he ended his life picking up the pieces of broken dreams—devastated by a catastrophic moral earthquake.

Have you known someone like Samson? Someone who had a good beginning? Someone who was God-anointed, God-appointed, and had every possible advantage in life, yet succumbed to the shock of a moral earthquake? _____ Name that person's initials. _____

Samson's experience confirms the lamentable fact that even a godly home is no absolute guarantee of a godly life. Sometimes our best-intended spiritual influences are rejected by our children. Some of us are eerily like Samson—we have been brought up in godly homes by parents who prayed for us, dedicated us, and sacrificed for us through the years; yet we choose to live our lives along the dangerous fault lines of sin and rebellion.

"Again the children of Israel did evil in the sight of the LORD, and the LORD delivered them into the hand of the Philistines for forty years. Now there was a certain man from Zorah, of the family of the Danites, whose name was Manoah; and his wife was barren and had no children. And the Angel of the LORD appeared to the woman and said, 'Indeed now you are barren and have borne no children, but you shall conceive and bear a son. Now therefore, please be careful not to drink wine or similar drink, and not to eat anything unclean. For behold, you shall conceive and bear a son, and no razor shall come upon his head, for the child shall be a Nazarite to God from the womb, and he shall begin to deliver Israel out of the hand of the Philistines'" (Judg. 13:1–5).

Why do you suppose children often reject their parents' spiritual guidance?

OUTWARD EVIDENCES

Samson was particularly advantaged spiritually. In fact, we are told that he was a "Nazarite" from his mother's womb. A Nazarite was someone peculiarly set apart for the work of God. He was distinguished in holiness by three vows he was to keep forever. First, he vowed to never drink wine or even to go near a vineyard where grapes or raisins were grown. Second, he vowed to never touch a dead animal, because he was to live a separated, holy life unsullied by the curse of death. Third, he vowed to never cut his hair (Num. 6:2–8).

Each of these vows outwardly represented an inward commitment to holiness and righteousness. They were intended to be the external symbols of an internal reality in his heart and life. When men and women saw a Nazarite walking down the street, they immediately recognized him as a man of commitment, a man of holy resolve. Sadly, Samson trivialized his status as a Nazarite early in his life.

Evaluating your daily routine, what things can you do to increase a sense of commitment and holy resolve in your life?

Read how Samson's moral fault manifested itself in Judges 14:1 (printed in the margin).

"Now Samson went down to Timnah as a young man and saw a woman in Timnah of the daughters of the Philistines" (Judg. 14:1).

The Philistines were pagans. They were the very oppressors God had raised up Samson to defeat. Yet there he was. Samson knew better, but still he went. That was his first mistake. According to the story, he "saw" one of the daughters of the Philistines. Right then and there he was smitten. He made his decision to abandon his high calling and to reject his righteous upbringing—entirely on the basis of his senses. It seems that he was completely dominated by the desires of his flesh. Notice he had never had a conversation with this woman. He had never even met her. Certainly, he had never gone into her home. He knew nothing about her except what she looked like. This was sheer, stark, base, fleshly, physical attraction.

Why does it seem so easy to break away from commitments we make to God and to others?

One Thing Leads to Another

Samson was where he should not have been—down there at Timnah, down there with the godless people, down there among the Philistines—and that led to his second big mistake.

"So he went up and told his father and mother, saying, 'I have seen a woman in Timnah of the daughters of the Philistines; now therefore, get her for me as a wife' " (Judg. 14:2).

Read Samson's second mistake in Judges 14:2, printed in the margin. Reflecting on this passage, what observations (good and bad) would you make about Samson?

_____

_____

Samson went back home and said, "Mom, I've found the one. Dad, go down there and get her for me." He was ready for his parents to begin arranging for a wedding—and he had yet to even meet his prospective bride. He was obviously moved by nothing more than sheer physical attraction.

Thus began the small cracks in his character—the little secret faults—that would one day erupt into a full-force moral earthquake. Of course Samson knew better—he was a Nazarite, but he persisted in his obstinate commitment to fleshly desires.

Read Samson's parents' reaction in the margin from Judges 14:3.

Samson's dad said, "Look, this isn't how you've been brought up. This isn't what we taught you. This isn't the law we've lived by. Couldn't you find a believer? Couldn't you find someone who loves the Lord? Couldn't you find someone of common faith that would be able to worship with you and help raise your children as you were raised?" But Samson would hear none of that. He was resolute in his worldly passion, "Get her for me. I know what I'm doing. I can handle this."

Samson decided that he knew what was best for him—and thus he rejected the clear mandates of God's law and the wise inclinations of his parents' counsel. Thus, the fault lines began to spread even further: "So Samson went down to Timnah with his father and mother, and came to the vineyards of Timnah" (Judg. 14:5).

"Then his father and mother said to him, 'Is there no woman among the daughters of your brethren, or among all my people, that you must go and get a wife from the uncircumcised Philistines?' And Samson said to his father, 'Get her for me, for she pleases me well' " (Judg. 14:3).

How does it typically work out when you act on what you think is best for yourself?

_____

Where did Samson go? The vineyards of Timnah! Almost without warning, the secret faults in Samson's life lead him to violate one of the basic vows of his Nazarite commitment. He was not to go anywhere near a vineyard. He was not even allowed to touch as much as a single raisin. Yet there he was, walking through the vineyard, flagrantly doing the very thing he had vowed he would never do.

The fact is, when we say no to God in one area of our lives, when we let a little fault begin to spread, we are well on our way toward a moral earthquake. One thing leads to another, and we find ourselves irretrievably on the downgrade. Thus complications began to mount almost immediately for Samson: "Now to his surprise, a young lion came roaring against him" (Judg. 14:5).

Briefly describe a decision you made that led to further complications.

_____

When we step out of God's will for our lives, we shouldn't be terribly surprised when we are confronted with obstacles. Samson thought he could avert disaster, but he actually only made things worse.

Read how Samson made things worse in Judges 14:6-7, printed in the margin.

Sin has consequences. We may be ingenious in our efforts to avoid those consequences—as Samson was when he faced the lion in the vineyard. But ultimately, even our best efforts at ingenuity are to no avail.

One sin leads to another. One compromise leads to the next. Samson very nearly met with disaster because he was where he never should have been, doing what he never should have been doing, with someone he never should have been with. Yet, lo and behold, at the very next opportunity he returned for more. It was almost as if he were winking at sin. He apparently thought he could get away with anything. Whenever we give in to sin, we pick up next time where we left off: "After some time, when he had returned to get her, he turned aside to see the carcass of the lion. And behold a swarm of bees and honey were in the carcass of the lion. He took some of it with his hands and went along, eating" (Judg. 14:8–9).

So, Samson returned to the vineyard. When he did, he turned aside to revisit his narrow escape; there he violated the second of his Nazarite vows—that he would not touch a dead body. Not only did Samson touch the carcass of the lion he had slain; he actually ate from it.

Samson was exactly like so many of us today. Carried along by the passions of the moment, he somehow forgot that actions always have consequences. Those consequences may not be immediate, but they are sure and certain nonetheless. It would be twenty years before Samson was entirely undone, but the stage was set in those vineyards of Timnah. The cracks in his character made the foundations of his life less secure. His secret faults—well hidden beneath the surface—made what seemed to be unimaginable, all too inevitable.

What passions of the moment have adversely affected your life?

Describe how you have felt the affects after succumbing to such passions.

_____

Twenty years later, Samson met Delilah. Then came the earthquake—and thus his life ended in ruin. Earthquakes don't just happen. They are always preceded by secret faults.

So it is with all of us. A marriage doesn't just fall apart. It is slowly and imperceptibly undermined over a long span of time by small infidelities, by little accommodations to dishonesty, and by seemingly harmless flirtations. These tiny fissures eventually become gaping chasms. These little cracks in the integrity of the relationship finally erupt into a catastrophic quake—bringing with it monumental destruction.

Similarly, ethical violations in the workplace, the fierce bondage of habitual immorality, and the sad descent into addictive behaviors all begin with small indiscretions but end in great devastation.

day Four

Powerful Aftereffects

As the residents of Lisbon discovered on that calamitous day in 1755, even an apparently minor tremor along a fault line can have ongoing, residual effects—one aftershock following another—that can ultimately usher in complete destruction. Moral earthquakes are very similar. They can have devastatingly destructive residual effects. Sometimes those effects are not manifested until sometime much later.

Moral earthquakes are thus not only preceded by secret faults; they are succeeded by sudden aftershocks. Witness again the sad saga of Samson.

THE DELILAH DILEMMA

You would think that somewhere along the way, Samson would have learned his lesson. Sadly though, his disappointing experiences with the Philistines only deepened the pattern of rebellion in his life, exacerbating

In 1755, the great Portuguese city of Lisbon was struck by a tremendous earthquake. Though powerful, it appeared that the initial damage was minimal. Then, after a few moments of calm, an aftershock hit. It lasted only two minutes but brought with it terrible devastation. Many older buildings broke apart. A number of roads buckled. Several wharves surrounding the busy port collapsed under the turbulent waters. Even so, most citizens breathed a sigh of relief. The worst was over—or so they thought. The land actually stilled only for a moment. Suddenly, another aftershock rocked the city for nearly 10 minutes. This time, almost everything in sight was left in a shambles. The once resplendent city was reduced to little more than a heap of ruins.

Yet there was more to come. The survivors had to face fires that had broken out all over the city. The few homes and buildings that remained standing were so unstable that even the slightest breeze threatened to topple them. As if all that were not enough, a succession of great waves caused by the quake began shattering the already decimated shoreline. Fifteen- to fifty-foot-high waves pounded into the rubble of the city three times.

Hundreds of panic-stricken people, waiting in the harbor to cross the sole remaining bridge over the Tagus River, were suddenly swept away. Almost two hours after the first tremors began, Lisbon continued to reel from the aftereffects of what at first seemed to be a rather trifling quake. By the end of the harrowing ordeal, an estimated 70,000 of the 275,000 people living in the city had died from the quake and its frightening succession of aftershocks.

the cracks in his character. He claimed belief in the ways of the Lord, but he didn't act like it. Meanwhile, he disclaimed the ways of the world but then conformed himself to them at every turn.

By the time Samson had his infamous encounter with the temptress Delilah, he had actually reinforced his impassioned rebellious habits for some twenty years. During that time, the character of Samson had become so damaged—so weakened by secret faults and cracks in his character—that he was unable to stop himself. Even in the face of obvious danger, he had become a slave to his passions.

How has being enslaved to something affected your decision-making capacity?

_____

You see, when we allow our secret faults to continue unarrested and unabated over the years, we lose the ability to exercise even the most basic elements of common sense. The fact is, when secret faults are left unarrested, we tend to lose all sense of propriety. We begin to do things we would never have done before, and the results are disastrous, as they were for Samson.

Read Samson's situation in Judges 16:4-5, printed in the margin of page 103.

Up to that time, though Samson had allowed secret faults to run all throughout his life, he had been a scourge to the dreaded Philistines. He disrupted their reign of terror among the people of Israel and became a champion of freedom. Now they saw an opportunity to exploit his obvious weakness for beautiful women. They came to his latest object of illicit affection, Delilah, and struck a bargain with her to betray him.

So Delilah came on to Samson and begged, "Please tell me where your great strength lies" (Judg. 16:6). Of course, she didn't just come right out and brazenly ask him to betray his secret. She enticed him first by inviting him into her lair. She wined and dined him. She utilized all of her provocative allure. She broke down his few remaining defenses, scruples, and inhibitions.

Read how the story ominously unfolded in that sensual setting in Judges 16:6-7, printed in the margin.

Having weakened Samson's sensibilities with raw physical passion, Delilah plied her question, "What is your secret?" Apparently though, Samson still had some of his wits about him and he lied to her. Delilah, intent on her betrayal, proceeded to bind about him "seven fresh bowstrings" while he slept (Judg. 16:8). Immediately after, she disingeniously cried out, "The Philistines are upon you." But when his attackers came out of hiding in the bed chamber to pounce on him, Samson surprised them all, sundered the bowstrings "as a thread of tow is broken when it toucheth the hearth fire," and then furiously smote them (Judg. 16:9, KJV).

DUMB AND DUMBER

Amazingly, Samson failed to learn from this betrayal and narrow escape. He was so smitten by his fleshly attraction to Delilah that he remained captive to her affections. The moral earthquake in his life had finally taken its toll. Now one aftershock followed another, bringing with them increasing ruin. In a very real sense, Samson went from dumb to dumber—just as we do when we become captive to our temptations.

What things entice us to come closer, even when we know they will harm us?

_____

Now read how Delilah, undeterred, pressed her ploy further in Judges 16:10-11, printed in the margins of pages 103-104.

Again, though Samson was toying with complete disaster, he kept his wits about him and deceived his lover. Once again Delilah called the Philistines out of hiding, and once again, Samson defeated them handily. Nevertheless, he allowed the farce to continue. His expedient accommodation to fleshly desire not only made a mockery of his calling and confession, it completely undermined the foundations of his life.

"Afterward it happened that he loved a woman in the Valley of Sorek, whose name was Delilah. And the lords of the Philistines came up to her, 'Entice him, and find out where his great strength lies, and by what means we may overpower him, that we may bind him to afflict him; and every one of us will give you eleven hundred pieces of silver' " (Judg. 16:4–5).

"Delilah said to Samson, 'Please tell me where your great strength lies, and with what you may be bound to afflict you.' And Samson said to her, 'If they bind me with seven fresh bowstrings, not yet dried, then I shall become weak, and be like any other man' " (Judg. 16:6–7).

"Then Delilah said to Samson, 'Look, you have mocked me and told me lies. Now, please tell me what you may be bound with.'

So he said to her, 'If they bind me securely with new ropes that have never been used, then I will become weak, and be like any other man' " (Judg. 16:10–11).

Delilah said to Samson, "Until now you have mocked me and told me lies. Tell me what you may be bound with." And he said to her, "If you weave the seven locks of my head into the web of the loom" (Judg. 16:13).

Do you see what was happening? Samson had weakened. One aftershock after another had left him practically defenseless. He came tantalizingly close to telling her the truth. He had become so overconfident that he thought he could get away with just about anything. That is what habitual sin always does to us.

So pulling out all the stops, Delilah said to him, "How can you say, 'I love you,' when your heart is not with me?" (Judg. 16:15). That line may be the oldest cliché in the book. It has been used in the moral collapse of more men, women, and young people than perhaps any phrase since the Fall. Though it is patently transparent, it is amazingly effective, isn't it? And thus, like so many before and so many since, Samson fell for it. Delilah pestered him with her cloying affections and maudlin sentiments until, finally, Samson's resistance was completely worn down and he relented.

What typically wears down your resistance?

_____

_____

Read Judges 16:17.

"No razor has ever come upon my head, for I have been a Nazarite to God from my mother's womb. If I am shaven then my strength will leave me, and I shall become weak, and be like any other man" (Judg. 16:17).

Even in the midst of his collapse, Samson could still articulate the truth. He still understood the essence and significance of his calling. Though he played into the hands of his own betrayal, though he left untended secret faults and cracks in his character for all those years, right up until the time of the whole collapse he could still speak the truth. Some people wonder how a man can stand in the pulpit or exercise authority in the home or take a public stand for righteousness when all the while immorality has begun to consume his mind, will, or emotions. Samson exemplified the greatest irony of sin in the life of a believer—he knew full well the difference between right and wrong, but he chose wrong anyway. Of his own volition, he rejected truth for a lie.

What can you hang on to in order to protect yourself from choosing a lie?

_____

Blind, Bound, and Belittled

That night, Samson's ruin was assured. Delilah cut away his long Nazarite braids—the final remnant of his righteous commitment was shorn from his life. "She said, 'The Philistines are upon you, Samson!' So he awoke from his sleep and said, 'I will go out as before, at other times, and shake myself free!' " (Judg. 16:20).

Why do you think Samson, even though his hair was cut, still thought he had the strength to fight the Philistines?

_____

Alas, Samson's demise was now complete. His moral faults had remained unexamined for so long that he was unaware of the full extent of the damages. His moral earthquake had wrecked havoc on the foundations of his life, and he didn't even know it. This final aftershock collapsed the tottering remains of his pride: "Then the Philistines took him and put out his eyes, and brought him down to Gaza. They bound him with bronze fetters, and he became a grinder in the prison" (Judg. 16:21).

At long last the consequences of Samson's profligate life were made evident. The great champion was left to grope in a shattered darkness, bound in chains, sentenced to grind the meal of his enemies, like some lowly ox. For years he had flaunted his dominion over his enemies while at the mercy of his base animal instincts. Now his enemies flaunted their dominion over him while he was forced to live out his final days as an animal. His humiliation was complete.

Samson was blind, bound, and belittled. For their parties the Philistines would bring him out to mock him and to mock God. That is just what sin ultimately does to all of us if we persist in it. It blinds us, it binds us, and it belittles us. It makes a mockery of us, and it makes a mockery of our God as well.

Samson lost his strength. He lost his sight. He lost his freedom. He lost his usefulness. He lost his testimony. He lost his reputation. He lost everything. But it didn't just happen. His great moral earthquake was preceded by secret faults. It was then succeeded by a whole host of sudden aftershocks.

Behind the business desks and the church desks all across this nation are men and women who for years have said, "I love the Lord Jesus Christ." Yet underneath their facade are unseen secret faults—cracks in character that one day will bring about a moral earthquake for all to see. The results will be no less catastrophic than they were in the life of the great Samson. Once the most powerful man of his day, Samson was reduced to practical irrelevance by his own foolish adherence to the ways of the flesh. This is what even the most trivial of sins can do to us. We think such things are really no big deal, but we are so wrong.

This ought to be a warning to us all. The end of Samson's life is a solemn reminder that there are consequences to sin. For twenty years, Samson assumed he could ignore all of the secret faults that lay beneath the surface of his life, but he was wrong. He thought he could get away with a few minor indiscretions from time to time, but he couldn't. We all tend to believe at one time or another that we can ignore our sins. But the fact remains, our sins will not ignore us.

Samson was utterly broken. Describe a time when you experienced a sense of brokenness.

_____

If you could go back, what actions and attitudes would you change to avert this season of brokenness?

_____

Before the Session

1. Consider researching on the Internet about earthquakes and fault lines. Any background information you can provide about this subject will be helpful as you interact with the earthquake imagery in Hawkins's material. If you run a search on the Internet, use the following words in your investigation: *seismology, plate tectonics, earthquakes, fault lines, and San Andreas Fault.*

2. Identify any individuals in your class who you know have experienced an earthquake or some other seismic activity. Prearrange for this person to share briefly about his or her experiences.

3. Have available large tear sheets, markers, and tape or tacks.

During the Session

1. Ask: *Has anyone ever experienced an earthquake?* Allow time for sharing. Take time to briefly describe the reason for an earthquake happening. Then transition discussion toward the topic of morality. Ask: *How does Dr. Hawkins compare our own moral struggles with an earthquake?* Encourage learners to point out the similarities. For further discussion refer to both interactive activities in Day 1.

2. Start by reading Judges 13:1-5. Say: *With all the positive support in his life, Samson made some bad decisions.* Then ask: *Why do you think this happened? Who was at fault?* Many learners can relate to the struggle of raising a child who turned out rebellious. Help learners recognize that raising a child "the right way" doesn't necessarily guarantee that the child will embrace what the parents have taught. For follow-up discussion regarding this point, use the second interactive activity in Day 2. Direct learners to read Judges 14:1. Allow learners to share how this verse reflects a bad choice in Samson's life. Follow with asking learners to share their responses to the fourth interactive activity in Day 2.

3. Read Judges 14:2-7. Ask learners to share the progression of decisions that Samson made. A key objective is to help learners identify how one bad decision leads to another bad choice. Ask: *How do our own bad decisions parallel Samson's folly?* Ask learners to share how they responded to the second interactive activity in Day 3. (**Note: Many of the**

To the Leader:

Discussing morality is tough. In one sense, it is a difficult subject because it hits at the heart of every person's struggle. Indeed, we all struggle with morality. Thus it is important in your teaching approach to establish a sense of ease for learners in your class. Emphasize that moral struggles are a relevant topic for everyone. We have all made poor decisions in life and need help navigating future moral challenges. In particular, make sure that no one moral issue becomes a sort of "easy target." It's easy to point at someone else's moral dilemma and divert attention away from our own struggles. Keep the focus on our common vulnerability with sin.

interactive questions in Day 3 are personal. Use sensitivity in discussion people's reactions to these questions.)

4. Read Judges 16:4-17. Together, summarize what happened in this particular passage. Encourage learners to compare this story to the way sin typically works itself out in our world today. Explain that Samson was "enslaved" to his passions. Ask: *What do we typically find ourselves enslaved to?* Also direct learners to consider what they can do to protect themselves from bad moral decisions. Discuss the fourth interactive question in Day 4.

5. Continue reading about Samson in Judges 16:18-21. Encourage learners to share how they responded to the first interactive activity in Day 5. After analyzing how Samson came to his tragic capture, direct learners to read the remainder of the story about Samson in Judges 16:22-31. Emphasize that Samson made some critically bad decisions, and he suffered. At the same time, emphasize that this wasn't the end of the story. God still used him. Allow learners to share how they have observed God taking broken people and using them again for great things.

6. Consider using a large sheet of paper for each week of this six-week study. Write on the top of the page *Living on the Fault Line*. Under this title, allow learners to list lessons learned from the life of Samson. Then, using a different colored marker, ask learners to come up with one "take-away" application that this lesson teaches about how to protect ourselves from a moral earthquake. After completing this exercise, post the paper on the wall. Each week repost the prior weeks' feedback to remind learners of what they are learning.

Fight and Flight

day One

Predictable Fault Lines

An earthquake can happen almost anywhere. Although this statement seems to defy what we know about plate tectonics, it is true. In 1818 a violent quake shook Missouri. In 1886 another struck South Carolina. In 1988 another ripped through Australia's Northern Territory, and in 1990 one hit Britain. As far as geophysicists can tell, there are no active plate boundaries in any of these areas. Scientists theorize that instability well below the top layer of the earth's crust—undetectable faults far deeper than the plate boundaries—may be the cause of this rare form of subduction.

The one solace of such phenomena is that they are, after all, rare. Even though it is *possible* for an earthquake to occur anywhere, it is far from *probable*. In fact, the vast majority of earthquakes occur along predictable fault lines along plate boundaries. They always have and they always will.

Moral earthquakes follow a similar pattern. Though it is possible for a moral earthquake to be caused by the most inconsequential moral faults, it is more likely to be caused by more predictable fault lines. In fact, the vast majority of moral earthquakes are caused by greed, avarice, bitterness, and, of course, sexual promiscuity.

Sex. We are consumed by it. We are immersed in it. We can hardly escape its smothering influences. Our entire pop culture seems to revolve around it. Yet our obsession has hardly brought us satisfaction. On the contrary, it has brought untold suffering and destruction.

List three ways you see sexuality misrepresented in our society.

1. _____

2. _____

3. _____

"Flee sexual immorality. Every sin that a man does is outside the body, but he who commits sexual immorality sins against his own body. Or do you not know that your body is the temple of the Holy Spirit who is in you, whom you have from God, and you are not your own? For you were bought at a price; therefore glorify God in your body and in your spirit, which are God's" (1 Cor. 6:18–20).

It is ironic that our sophisticated society cannot see that sexual immorality has devastated our culture. The evidence is glaring: millions of illegitimate births, the highest divorce rate in the world, rampant sexually transmitted diseases—including AIDS—not to mention an unchecked abortion industry that not only victimizes preborn children, it haunts millions of women with the plague of post-abortion syndrome.

Yet we are continually bombarded with sex, sex, and more sex. We can't pick up a newspaper, a magazine, turn on a television set, go to a movie, or see an advertisement without salvos of innuendo, bravado, and libido. Sex sells in America. It sells blue jeans. It sells music. It sells mouthwash. It sells everything: cars, computers, and cameras. As a result, yesterday's shocking behavior is quite commonplace today.

To make matters worse, we've raised a generation of young people, by and large, with no moral absolutes and no spiritual leadership at home or in the church. Almost everyone talks to them about sex—except moms and dads and pastors. Consequently, a generation of kids have learned about sex from Madonna and the media, from public education and the Dr. Ruths of this world who fill their young minds with misinformation and half-truths.

In the church, these young people have stood by and watched as we steadfastly avoided addressing the most critical issues of our day. At the same time, however, they observed all too many high-profile leaders of the church fall into sexual sins.

Is it any wonder that so many young people succumb to these sexual pressures and temptations when the home, the church, and the nation fail to give them the moral support they need? We've raised a generation without moral absolutes because in school, at home, and in the church our young people are not hearing the whole story. There's only one way to have safe sex—the Bible's way.

America is in the midst of moral collapse and we're asking, "What should we do about it?" Many say, "More education. Distribute condoms. Find a cure." However, what we really ought to be asking is *why?* Why are we standing idly by watching our culture fall into decay and disintegration?

On the scale on the top of page 111, circle your opinion for how well sexuality is represented within each category.

In the Media

Unhealthy   Neutral   Healthy

In the Church

Unhealthy   Neutral   Healthy

In Educational Institutions

Unhealthy   Neutral   Healthy

By the Government

Unhealthy   Neutral   Healthy

The Apostle Paul confronted this issue head-on when he wrote to a church of men and women living in a society in every way as perverted as ours. He didn't back away from this indelicate subject—because he knew how important it was. He said, "Flee sexual immorality. Every sin that a man does is outside the body, but he who commits sexual immorality sins against his own body. Or do you not know that your body is the temple of the Holy Spirit who is in you, whom you have from God, and you are not your own? For you were bought at a price; therefore glorify God in your body and in your spirit, which are God's" (1 Cor. 6:18–20).

When you read 1 Corinthians 6:18-20, what seems most relevant to your life?

_____

What questions does this passage raise in your mind?

_____

There are four things Paul lays out in this passage. There is *an admonition*: The faithful must flee from sexual immorality. There is *an addition*: Sexual sin directly alters our lives. There is *an admission*: We are not our own. And finally, there is *an ambition*: We are therefore to glorify God in our bodies.

Admonition

Notice the force and urgency of Paul's exhortation, his admonition. He states very plainly, "Flee sexual immorality."

Don't misunderstand what Paul is saying here. He is not saying to flee sex. Some people think to even mention the word is ugly and naughty. On the contrary, within the marriage relationship sex is beautiful, pure, and good. The Bible is absolutely clear on this point. It is a magnificent and joyous experience when placed within the boundaries God affords. Only when we wrench sex out of its God-ordained parameters does it become evil, perverted, and divisive.

How have you seen sex depicted within the context of the church?

For the Christian the issue is not sex per se. It is sex outside God's design. The apostle does not say, "Flee sex"; he says, "Flee sexual immorality." Christians are not antisex. We simply have a higher view of it than it being mere animal instinct.

The real issue here is immorality. The Greek word for "immorality" is *porneia,* the same root from which we get the word *pornography. Porneia* appears a dozen times in the New Testament, and in each instance it refers to illicit sexual encounters outside a husband-wife relationship. Sometimes that illicit activity is fornication. Sometimes it is adultery. Sometimes it is homosexuality. All illicit sexual activity outside the sacred marital bed of a husband and wife is a perversion of God's perfect plan and providence.

Therefore the apostle asserts that whenever temptations in this arena present themselves, we are to flee. In the original Greek text, there is a present imperative in this admonition. It means we shouldn't weigh our options or consider alternatives. In the face of sexual temptation, we are to flee. Literally, we are to run rapidly away—without hesitation, without consideration, without consultation. We are simply to flee. The same word is used in Matthew's account of the infancy of Christ when Mary and Joseph took the baby Jesus and fled down to Egypt. They ran away when Herod decreed that all the babies in Bethlehem two years of age and younger would be killed. The same word is found later when Christ's followers ran away in fear following His arrest: "All the disciples forsook Him and fled" (Matt. 26:56). In its every occurrence, the word means immediate departure, flight, a quick escape.

So Paul's admonition is not simply to avoid sexual sin. We are to consciously, purposely, and perpetually run away from it. Get away. Run. Flee. Don't even get in a situation where sexual impropriety is possible. Flee.

Why do you think Paul used the word "flee"?

_____

Some of us try to fight this kind of temptation. We try to resist it thinking, *Oh, I'm strong. I can handle this situation. I've never fallen yet. I can fight these temptations.* To this, the Apostle Paul simply says, "Let him who thinks he stands take heed lest he fall" (1 Cor. 10:12).

Paul doesn't say, "*Fight* sexual immorality." Nor does he say, "Muster your faith in the face of sexual temptation." We might think, *Well, I'm a Christian; I know the Bible; I've lived a life of faith. I'll just exercise my faith here.*

Sadly, I've watched several friends in the ministry stumble into sexual immorality, and I've seen the catastrophic results in both their personal and professional lives. Invariably, they were men who thought they had the faith to avoid such a moral earthquake.

That is why Paul is entirely unambiguous here. His admonition is crystal clear: "Flee sexual immorality." Get out of there. Run. Don't hesitate. Don't weigh the situation. Don't stop to consider your options. Don't even pause to pray about it. Just get out of there. Flee. When you feel the temptations of the flesh, get out of there!

Addition

The reason we are to flee is simple: Sexual immorality brings devastation to all three types of relationships in life—with others, with ourselves, and with God. Sexual immorality affects your worth, your witness, and your worship. It adds an unnecessary dimension of tragedy and destruction to our lives.

How have you observed the effects of immorality impact the following relationships? Respond to as many as are applicable.

Others: _____

Yourself: _____

God: _____

Men and women often have different reasons for engaging in illicit sexuality. By and large, women give sex to get love. Many young ladies have never known a father's love. Their souls cry out for someone to love them. So they give their bodies away looking for love.

Men do the opposite. They give love to get sex. To satisfy themselves, they say, "I love you." Yet what they are often saying is, "I love me," and consequently, "I want you to satisfy me." It just comes out "I love you."

Tragically, many teenagers have never witnessed the loving relationship of a husband and wife. They have never seen firsthand a marriage that defies worldly logic. They have never seen a man love his wife like Christ loved the church nor known a woman willing to love and submit to her husband. The end result is that both men and women feel brutally betrayed and utterly unsatisfied in their most intimate relations.

All too often the church is quick to say, "Don't do it. Just say no. Flee sexual immorality," yet we neglect to tell kids and adults why they should abstain from sex until marriage. Well, the Apostle Paul was not that inconsistent. He said, "Every sin that a man does is outside the body, but he who commits sexual immorality sins against his own body" (v. 18).

In the margin, paraphrase 1 Corinthians 6:18 in your own words. Why do you think Paul set sexual sin apart as unique?

_____

Sexual sin is unlike other sins because it adds consequences to life that other sins don't. Sexual sin marks us and masters us. This type of sin defines us and dominates us. It takes over our minds.

Other kinds of sin make us unclean externally, but sexual sin pollutes us internally. It adds a dimension of destructiveness to our lives—and thus inevitably heralds moral earthquakes like no other sins possibly could.

day Four

Admission

The Apostle Paul does not stop with an admonition and an addition. He next proffers an admission: "Do you not know that your body is the temple of the Holy Spirit who is in you, whom you have from God, and you are not your own? For you were bought at a price" (vv. 19–20).

In the New Testament there are two different words that we translate "temple." The first refers to the entire temple complex in Jerusalem—the temple mount, the court of the Gentiles, Solomon's portico, the colonnades, and all the inner courts. The other word is used exclusively for the sacred space just behind the altar and beyond the veil in the inner court—the Holy of Holies. When Paul says, "Your body is the temple," he uses that second word. He asserts that a believer's body is the most holy place, the dwelling place of the Holy Spirit. It is God's Holy of Holies.

How often does the phrase "Holy of Holies" best describe the way you see your body? Mark your response on the continuum.

Never   **Often**

Why do you feel this way? _____

In the Old Testament God came to the temple and dwelt in that holy place. The *shekinah* glory of God inhabited that space between the cherubim over the mercy seat of the ark in the Holy of Holies. Now, in this dispensation, He says that the believer's body is that sacred place.

Even if we should ever become involved in illicit sexual sin, most of us would never think of committing it in a holy place. We would never think of desecrating a church, for instance. We would never flaunt our brazenness so profligately. Nor would we ever think of going into a beautiful cathedral or a great sanctuary in Bethlehem and committing sexual sin there. In a much more vivid and biblical way, we should recoil at the thought of committing such sin at all, regardless of the place or the geography. God doesn't inhabit a building or a plot of ground or a historic site. He inhabits His temple, and the believer's body is that temple. We shouldn't anymore think about sexual sin outside the parameters of God's Word in our body than we would in any holy place. Our bodies are, in fact, the only genuinely holy places in the created order.

The truth is, our bodies are not our own, and we have no right to injure property that does not belong to us. God bought us at great price.

Realizing that you were "bought at a price," what needs to immediately change as far as the way you treat your body?

_____

_____

Ambition

Finally, the Apostle Paul portrays an appropriate ambition for our lives: "Therefore, glorify God in your body and in your spirit, which are God's" (v. 20).

What should be our ambition in life? Should it be to satisfy our own personal whims, our own personal desires, our own personal expectations? Or should it be to glorify Jesus Christ?

Paul makes the case clearly: We ought to glorify God in all that we are and all that we do. He states this mandate in the strongest possible language. This sentence is even cast in the imperative mood. This is not an option for the believer. We are to radiate the life of Christ and His ownership of us with our whole being—including our bodies. In every way, in every matter, in every manner, we are to glorify God.

Yet how can we glorify God in our bodies? When we come face-to-face with temptation, there are three questions we should ask.

The first question is "Can I thank God for it?" The Bible says, "In everything give thanks; for this is the will of God in Christ Jesus for you" (1 Thess. 5:18). At every temptation, I ask myself, "If I go ahead and do this, can I look back after it's done and thank God for it?" If not, then I need to flee. I need to get out of there.

The second question is this: "Can I do it in Jesus' name?" The Bible says, "Whatever you do in word or deed, do all in the name of the Lord Jesus" (Col. 3:17). I ask myself, "If I go ahead and do this, will I actually be able to do it in Jesus' name?" If not, then I need to flee. I need to get out of there.

The third and final question is "Can I do it for God's glory?" The Bible says, "Therefore whether you eat or drink, or whatever you do, do it all to the glory of God" (1 Cor. 10:31). I ask myself, "Can I possibly do this for God's glory?" If not, then I need to flee. I need to get out of there.

God calls us to purity of mind, morals, motives, and marriages. Paul's words of admonition, addition, admission, and ambition offer us a glorious hope—and a way to avoid the devastation of the innumerable moral earthquakes of our time.

Identify a troubling temptation within your life and evaluate this issue utilizing the three questions referenced in today's discussion. Write your responses below:

My issue: _____

Can I thank God for it? _____

Can I do it in Jesus' name? _____

Can I do it for God's glory? _____

Before the Session

1. Study the background of the Corinthian church. A good resource for background information is the *Illustrated Holman Bible Dictionary*, which is both in printed form and also accessible as an online resource (visit resources at *www.Lifeway.com* to access this dictionary). Corinth was a sexually explosive place during the era when Paul was living. With that said, the people in the Corinthian church struggled with sexuality in many ways that our present day culture struggles with the subject.

2. Have available large tear sheets, markers, and tape or tacks.

During the Session

1. Point out that sexuality is a genuine battlefield when it comes to morality. Ask learners to share how they responded to the first and second interactive activities in Day 1 (or provide time for them to complete the activities). Instruct learners to read 1 Corinthians 6:18-20. Ask learners to share how they responded to the third interactive activity in Day 1.

2. Dr. Hawkins emphasized that sexuality is a beautiful gift from God. Ask learners to react to this statement. Utilize the first interactive activity of Day 2 to facilitate discussion of how sexuality has been addressed in their experiences within the church. Ask: *If sex is such a positive and wonderful thing, why can it also be so devastating?* Instruct learners to look at Paul's advice in 1 Corinthians 6:18-20. Ask: *What was Paul's advice, as far as dealing with sexual immorality?* Encourage learners to share how you can learn to "flee" from sexually compromising situations.

3. Ask learners to share how they responded to the first interactive activity in Day 3. Help learners understand that distorted sexuality has a devastating effect on our total well-being. Reread 1 Corinthians 6:18. Ask: *How does this verse serve to protect us from making a bad moral decision?*

4. Ask learners to share how they responded to the first interactive activity in Day 4 (or give them time to complete the activity). If helpful, emphasize to learners that the Holy of Holies reflected an extreme closeness to God's presence. God has an extremely high view of us. God wants us to see ourselves as His valuable possessions. We must treat ourselves with the utmost care.

To the Leader:

Sexuality is an important topic! Churches ought to be the one place in society where people are presented with a positive and encouraging view of sexuality. With that said, you need to gauge how you will approach the subject. Some in your class may be very uncomfortable discussing the subject simply because they are not used to talking about sex in a church context (or any other setting for that matter). Don't try to shock or force people to discuss sexual issues. Simply allow your group to dialogue at a level that feels comfortable to them. Be sensitive to the fact that many of those in your class likely may have struggled with sexuality at some point in their lives. Make sure your group discusses this topic with a lot of grace!

5. Explain that temptations are an ever-present part of all our lives. Thus we need guidance concerning how we can combat temptation. Have learners reread 1 Corinthians 6:18-20. Ask: *What does this passage offer, as far as helpful counsel, when it comes to combating temptation?* Ask learners to look back through Day 5 and identify the three questions Dr. Hawkins offered as a way to think through temptations we face. Challenge learners to consider how they can utilize these questions as they face temptations in the coming week.

6. Using another large sheet of paper for this week of the six-week study, write on the top of the page the words *Fight and Flight.* Allow learners to list under this title some lessons learned from your discussion and particularly from 1 Corinthians 6:18-20. Then, using a different colored marker, ask learners to come up with one "take-away" application that this lesson teaches about how to protect one's self from a moral earthquake. After completing this exercise, post the paper on the wall. Each week, repost the prior weeks' feedback to remind learners what they are learning.

Moral Intersections

Turning Point

The earthquake that struck the San Francisco Bay area in 1989 collapsed a section of the freeway that connects the cities of Oakland and San Francisco—including a long span of double-decked viaduct. The results were horrifying. Not only were hundreds of motorists injured and stranded in the immediate aftermath of the quake, but precarious driving conditions continued in the region for weeks and months afterward. Even after the rubble had been removed, the weakened bridges demolished, and the damaged pavement barricaded, hazards abounded for drivers.

Just imagine: The entire roadway system was altered overnight. Streets ceased to be passable; traffic light operations, rush-hour flow patterns, and contraflow schemes were all disrupted; one-way streets suddenly had to accommodate two-way traffic; and residential streets became primary arteries. Detours became the norm rather than the exception. Wrong turns were common occurrences.

Briefly describe an experience that abruptly altered the daily rhythm of your life.

_____

_____

_____

As a father, I was determined to teach my girls at least five basic lessons about driving. The first was read your map and know the directions to your destination ahead of time. In other words, I didn't want them to get to a major intersection and not know which way to turn. The second lesson I taught them was stop when you see a red light. Now that sounds pretty simplistic, but simple rules are generally the best rules. Besides, it is absolutely amazing how many motorists ignore this common-sense dictum. The third lesson I taught my girls was yield the right of way to others. The fourth lesson was submit to the proper authorities. Obey all the traffic signs. Obey the police. When we remain under authority, we will inevitably be safer. The fifth lesson I taught my girls was look both ways before you go. But when you go, really go. Don't hesitate in the middle of an intersection. Look both ways, and when it's clear, go on your way.

Clearly, these five lessons are basic to roadway protocol, but they are equally applicable to all our other everyday affairs—to our moral journeys through this life.

Life has unexpected twists, turns, and intersections as well. Though they come at different times for each of us, they are strikingly similar—each involves a moral decision we must make. At every intersection we must decide which way to go, and a wrong turn at a moral intersection of life can affect our journey for a lot of miles. Some people who make a wrong turn at a moral intersection spend years of their lives getting nowhere on side streets, cul-de-sacs, and dead ends. Others end up having wrecks that cause hurt and damage to others. At these moral intersections of life, the question isn't whether to turn right or left; the question is whether to turn *right* or *wrong*.

Joseph came to a moral intersection of life as a relatively young man. He was forced to take the wheel and drive himself. Up until this time his dad had made many of his decisions for him. Yet when we read about Joseph's situation in Potiphar's house, we find him in a precarious situation—at a moral intersection.

The road that brought him to this particular intersection was filled with all kinds of mountaintops and valleys. He drove on the mountaintop for a while as the favorite son of his father, receiving from him the fabled coat of many colors. Later, he had a dream in which God revealed to Joseph His plan for his life. He knew what God wanted him to do. He was to be the leader of a great nation. So Joseph cruised along with the top down, enjoying the beautiful view as he drove over the mountaintop. Suddenly his journey took him down into the valley.

Because of the jealousy and hatred of his brothers, Joseph was thrown into a pit and later sold. His slavery to the Ishmaelites took him down into Egypt. His journey descended even farther into the valley. He was sold on a block and purchased by a man named Potiphar who made him his personal slave—a servant in his home.

Eventually Joseph's character and integrity caused him to be made ruler over all of Potiphar's home. He was young, bright, intelligent, and powerful. He was riding high again, but it was not to last. Shortly thereafter, he arrived at a great moral intersection.

Read Genesis 39:7-10, printed in the margin.

Notice Joseph not only resisted her seductions but he also didn't even want to be in the same vicinity as Potiphar's wife.

Read what happened next in Genesis 39:11-12, printed in the margin.

Joseph got out of there as fast as he possibly could. Potiphar's wife ripped the very shirt off his back. Then, to cover her own sin, she said he had tried to rape her. She falsely accused him. As a result of this accusation, Potiphar had Joseph thrown into an Egyptian dungeon. Joseph came to another moral intersection. Amazingly, he put into practice those same five principles I taught my daughters when they were first learning to drive.

Where in life do you often face moral intersections?

_____

How can you practically navigate these "intersections" in an appropriate way?

_____

_____

"It came to pass after these things that his master's wife cast longing eyes on Joseph, and she said, 'Lie with me.' But he refused and said to his master's wife, 'Look, my master does not know what is with me in the house, and he has committed all that he has to my hand. There is no one greater in this house than I, nor has he kept back anything from me, but you, because you are his wife. How then can I do this great wickedness, and sin against God?' So it was, as she spoke to Joseph day by day, that he did not heed her, to lie with her or to be with her" (Gen. 39:7–10).

"But it happened about this time, when Joseph went into the house to do his work, and none of the men of the house was inside, that she caught him by the garment, saying, 'Lie with me.' But he left his garment in her hand, and fled and ran outside" (Gen. 39:11–12).

day Two

Read the Map

Read the map and know your directions beforehand. When I taught my daughters to drive, I wanted them to think ahead, to know which way they were going to turn when they arrived at any given intersection. The reason is simple: If we are driving along in the far right lane and suddenly find ourselves at an intersection where we need to make an immediate left, we will need to maneuver through three or four lanes of on-rushing traffic to make the correct turn. We thus get into all kinds of problems and confusion. We bring confusion to others. We may even have a wreck. Sometimes we make wrong turns and are then loathe to ask for help. What is it about us that when we get lost or we make a wrong turn, we just won't ask anybody for directions? How many times has that kind of scenario been repeated in our lives?

What makes you hesitant to ask for guidance and direction?

Notice Joseph. He had already decided which way he was going to turn before he got to that moral intersection. Years before, God gave him a dream. God revealed to Joseph that He was going to use him in a mighty way. Joseph made some decisions in his own heart, and in his own life. As a result, the Bible tells us that "the Lord was with Joseph" (Gen. 39:2). That is why he became successful.

Joseph made the right turn at that intersection of life because he had already decided—he knew the route, and he had determined which way he was going to turn before he even got there. Joseph didn't stand in the intersection of Mrs. Potiphar's passion, ring his hands, and say, "Well, what should I do? Should I, or should I not?" He'd already made up his mind, before he ever got to that intersection. Unfortunately, many of us make wrong turns in life because we wait until we get into the middle of the intersection before we decide what we're going to do.

What do you think it means to make a decision in the "middle of the intersection"?

_____

Is this a wise practice? _____

Remember Samson? He made some wrong turns early in life. The rest of his life was spent on side streets, cul-de-sacs, and dead ends. Interestingly, Samson and Joseph had a lot in common. But what made the difference between these two young men was that when they came to moral intersections in life, one turned the right way and one turned the wrong way. But why? They both were blessed with striking personalities and good looks. In fact, the narrative says Joseph was handsome in form and appearance, and we know Samson was strapping, virile, athletic, and comely.

We read of both of them that "the Lord was with them." They both found themselves away from home in the midst of ungodly people—Samson amidst the Philistines, Joseph with the Egyptians—living in hostile environments. They even faced similar temptations—immoral relations with powerful, persistent, tempestuously seductive women.

Yet in nearly identical circumstances, we find that one turned right at that intersection and one turned wrong. Why? What was the difference?

As we said before, Joseph had already decided which way he was going to turn before he got there. Samson hadn't. He got in the middle of the intersection with Delilah, and she kept coming back. He didn't know what he was going to do, so he didn't do anything for a while. He was indecisive. He stood there for a time until finally he allowed his flesh to direct his way. He made a last-second turn—in the wrong direction.

Joseph's decision, on the other hand, is the kind of common sense resolve all of us need to exercise. Make a promise to God, to yourself, to your parents, to your future husband, to your future wife, or to your future children. Draw a line, and set your mind to it. Draw a line in your heart and your mind, and don't cross it. Then some Friday night when you get out into that moral intersection and see your friends turning the wrong way, you will know what you are going to do long before you even get there. You won't need to panic or freeze in indecision. You will have already decided the right turn.

That was one of the secrets of Joseph's life. Read the map, and know the directions beforehand.

Briefly summarize how Joseph "read the map."

_____

What is one way you can apply this principle to your own moral intersections?

_____

day Three

Just Say No

The second lesson Joseph applied was *stop when you see a red light.* "[Potiphar's] wife cast longing eyes on Joseph, and she said, 'Lie with me.' But he refused" (Gen. 39:7–8).

Stop when you see a red light. What an important lesson! How many people have been hurt because some driver was in such a big hurry that he or she ran through a red light? The driver thought he wouldn't get caught. She thought no police were around or he thought he could get by with it.

It's dangerous to run a red light, especially at moral intersections. Joseph was an overcomer because he said no from the start. The first time Potiphar's wife came to him he didn't flirt with her, think it was cute, or say, "Well, I'll never get into this, but I'll just play around with it awhile and see how far she takes it." No, he said no from the very beginning. He refused. When he saw that red light flashing, he stopped.

One of the most important words in any language is *no.* Joseph knew that. As a result, he refused. He was able to stand firm because he was unwavering from the start. That little two-letter word is the secret to overcoming many of the temptations we face in this life.

Now don't think Joseph wasn't tempted here. He was away from home in a foreign country, lonely, and with little to lose. He had no family there to embarrass or a reputation to maintain or defend; nobody knew him. He was also young and handsome. Potiphar's wife was a woman of power and undoubtedly a woman of beauty. Her seductions certainly would have appealed to his pride and fed his ego. It seemed like everybody else in the culture around him was already turning at similar moral intersections. He should have been flattered, many of his peers would have told him. But he knew how to say an important word—*no*. Why? Because he had already decided which way he was going to turn before he got there, and he stopped when he saw a red light.

But Potiphar's wife wouldn't take no for an answer. She came back day after day. Still, Joseph did not heed her. He didn't even want to be near her. He stayed out of her vicinity.

Describe in one sentence the "red light" for Joseph.

_____

What "red lights" show up in your daily routine?

_____

Some of us are foolish enough to think that we can flirt with sensual desires, that we can joke and kid about them, without actually being affected by them. For instance, think about what our kids are watching on television these days. We might say, "Oh, we don't have cable. We don't have HBO or MTV or anything like that." But what about ABC, NBC, CBS, and FOX?

How would Joseph have responded at that moral intersection if every night for hours on end that's what he'd been filling his mind with? Do we wonder at the explosion of teenage sexual sin today? Sadly, statistics indicate that Christian kids are about as involved in immorality as the other kids are.

Joseph was able to resist temptation because he took a strong stand from the very first. He knew which way he was going to turn. When he saw a red light, he stopped and said no.

Describe things in and around your life that have the potential for wearing you down and making you vulnerable to sin. Then indicate what you can do about them.

_____

_____

Yield the Right of Way

There is a third lesson Joseph learned: *Yield the right-of-way to others.* Certainly, that is an important lesson when we are learning to drive. Have respect for the other drivers. Be considerate to those around you. Give way to them. Yield to those who have the right-of-way.

At Joseph's moral intersection he showed respect for three people: first for Potiphar, second for himself, and finally for Potiphar's wife.

"Look," he said, "My master does not know what is with me in the house, and he's committed all that he has in my hands." Joseph respected Potiphar. He respected his position as a husband. He considered how Potiphar would feel if he found out that his trusted servant had carried on an affair with his wife. He valued Potiphar's friendship. As a result, he refused to steal the affection that was due Potiphar from his own wife.

Joseph also respected himself. "There's no one greater in this house," he asserted, "nor has he kept back anything from me." Joseph had too much respect for the integrity of his faith and commitment to the Lord to defile his body in an adulterous, illicit affair. He had too much self-respect to indulge in that kind of perversity. One of the things that we jettison when we make wrong turns at moral intersections is self-respect.

Joseph simply had too much regard for what God had confirmed and established in his life to yield to temptation in that sordid fashion.

Finally, Joseph demonstrated respect for Potiphar's wife. He respected her enough to say no to her advances. He said no because "you are his wife." He was able to clearly distinguish the difference between lust and love. Lust often comes disguised as love, but it is just a disguise. Love has the other person's highest ideal in mind. Joseph knew that, so he said no.

Based on the concept of "yielding the right of way" and with regard to your zones of temptation, whom do you need to yield to?

_____

Why will yielding to this particular individual protect you from compromising morality?

_____

Submit to Authority

The fourth lesson Joseph learned was *submit to the proper authorities.* That is what I tried to teach my daughters when they were first learning to drive. They were to obey the law. I told them that when they saw a traffic sign, they were to obey it. If they were, by chance, stopped by a police officer, they were to show him respect and submit to him as an authority that God ordained and appointed over us.

Notice how Joseph followed this basic mandate: "How then can I do this great wickedness, and sin against God?" he asked. Joseph recognized that, ultimately, all sin is rebellion against God. All breaches of conduct are an affront to His authority in our lives. All moral lapses are slights against Him—and Him only.

When you face moral decisions, how often do you employ God's guidance? ❑ **Never** ❑ **Often**

Where in particular do you most need an awareness of God's presence?

In the final analysis, it is our love for God that keeps us from turning the wrong way at the moral intersections of life. When we find ourselves in a situation where we are unlikely to get caught, where no one will know, often it is only our relationship with the Lord Jesus Christ that can keep us from turning the wrong way. This is the one thing that can keep us pure.

Does the fact that our involvement with sin is an affront against God ever come to mind? Why not? Is it because we have persistently refused to nurture a conscious awareness that He is always with us? Joseph was certainly aware of this danger. Thus throughout this text we find that "the Lord was with him."

What is one way you can increase an awareness of God's presence in your life?

Why don't some of us have a conscious awareness of God's presence with us? Perhaps it is because we constantly fill our minds with sensuality from television, movies, and music—and seldom with the Word of God. One of Joseph's secrets was that he lived a life conscious of the awareness of God.

Look Both Ways

Why do you suppose we sometimes move slowly through our temptation experiences?

Joseph's final lesson was *look both ways and then go*. I taught my daughters: When you get to the intersection, look both ways; then, if the coast is clear, don't hesitate out there—go on through the intersection. Notice that Joseph didn't try to fight his temptation. He fled it. He got out of there. Potiphar's wife ran up, grabbed him, and said, "Lie with me." But Joseph left his garment in her hand and ran out the door. He lost his coat, but he kept his character. He lost his vest, but he kept his virginity. He looked both ways, and he got out of there. Look both ways, and go.

How does 1 Corinthians 10:13 in a practical way serve to encourage us as we face difficult temptations?

The Bible says, "No temptation has overtaken you except such as is common to man; but God is faithful, who will not allow you to be tempted beyond what you are able, but with the temptation will also make an escape, that you may be able to bear it" (1 Cor. 10:13). Moral intersections in life are inevitable. We all get there sooner or later. The only question is, Which way are we going to turn? If we learn from Joseph and apply these principles to our own lives, then what was said of him might be said of us, "The Lord was with Joseph, and he was a successful man" (Gen. 39:2).

Before the Session

1. Joseph's story is remarkable. Read Genesis 37 and 39–48 for the purpose of understanding Joseph's total story. When approaching this lesson, it will be helpful to give a brief background concerning the life of Joseph.

2. This lesson affords an opportunity to apply Dr. Hawkins's suggestions to a case study that is relevant to the everyday context of your learners. Consider allowing learners to describe a moral dilemma that can be used for discussion purposes throughout the lesson. However, recognizing the possibility that learners may not come up with a "dilemma" of their own, come to class prepared with your own scenario that can be introduced as part of the class.

3. Have available large tear sheets, markers, and tape or tacks.

4. Bring a road map to class.

During the Session

1. Read Genesis 39 aloud as a class. After reading, allow learners to point out all the different circumstances of Joseph's life. Ask: *What moral intersections did Joseph face? Did Joseph have reason to give up on God and do whatever he wished? Why do you suppose he chose to maintain his integrity?* Allow time for discussion. Ask learners to describe how they responded to the second interactive activity in Day 1. After learners share examples of "moral intersections," ask the group to pick one and use it for a case study throughout the remainder of this lesson.

2. Bring in an example of a road map. Ask learners to share about a time when they felt a road map was most helpful. Ask learners to share about a time when they wished they had used a map but didn't. Ask: *In the material for Day 2, how did Dr. Hawkins use the map concept?* Ask learners to share how they responded to the third interactive activity of Day 2. Emphasize how Joseph "read the map" in his situation. Refer to the "moral intersection" you have chosen for a case study. Ask: *How should we "read the map" in this particular situation?*

3. Ask learners to share how they responded to the first interactive activity in Day 3 (or give them time to complete it). Direct attention back to the

To the Leader:

In this session Dr. Hawkins offers a terrific method for combating moral intersections that potentially can destroy our lives. The story of Joseph shows how we can live with integrity in this world of temptations. Learners constantly deal with the potential for moral compromise all around them. Joseph's story can serve as an encouragement that we can indeed live with integrity in this world.

131

"moral intersection" your class picked. Discuss how to apply the "stop at a red light" principal to this situation.

4. Ask: *Based on Dr. Hawkins's discussion, what does it mean to "yield the right of way"? How did Joseph do this?* Refer to the interactive for Day 4. Ask learners to share their responses. Then allow learners to consider to whom they would need to "yield the right of way" regarding the selected case study.

5. Explain that it is crucial to submit to authority when we think of moral intersections. Allow learners to explain what it means to submit to authorities, as described in this week's lesson. Ask: *How did Joseph model this principle?* Refer to the first and second interactive activities for Day 5 for further discussion and application. (**Note: The second activity for Day 5 is at the top of the column on page 130.**) Then ask learners to consider how they would apply this information to the case study situation.

6. Ask learners to explain what Dr. Hawkins meant by "look both ways and then go." Then ask learners to share how they responded to the last interactive of Day 5 in column on page 130. Emphasize that getting through a moral intersection as quick as possible is crucial. Read aloud as a group 1 Corinthians 10:13. Ask learners to consider how this verse encourages us in our battle with temptation. Now apply the "look both ways and then go" principle to your group's case study.

7. Using a large sheet of paper, write on the top of the page the words *Moral Intersections*. Under this title allow learners to list lessons they learned from today's discussion and particularly from Joseph's story in Genesis 39. Then, using a different colored marker, ask learners to come up with one "take-away" application that this lesson teaches about how to protect one's self from a moral earthquake. After completing this exercise, post the paper on the wall with those from the former lessons to remind learners what they are learning.

Restoring Joy

David's Two Requests

The red tape of bureaucracy drove the official in charge of rebuilding the earthquake-shattered city of Kobe to commit suicide. Government spokesmen reported that Deputy Mayor Takumi Ogawa—who was in charge of reconstructing the city after the worst natural disaster in Japan in the 20th century—set himself on fire after a frustrating year of rebuilding. Local officials had long criticized the central government for being too slow to respond to the disaster with money to help the city recover. Apparently Ogawa simply was unable to see how things would—or even could—get better.

Have you ever been in a situation where you didn't see things getting any better? _____

Anyone who has ever suffered a moral earthquake can sympathize. There is a kind of smothering grief that attends such a disaster. Often the aftermath can be as bad or worse than the original event.

Read and reacquaint yourself with David's moral earthquake in 2 Samuel 11:1—12:25 and Psalm 51:1-19 as background for this lesson.

It's not surprising then to see David crying out to God—in the aftermath of his moral earthquake—to bring him relief from his unrelenting agony: "Restore to me the joy of Your salvation, and uphold me by Your generous Spirit" (Ps. 51:12).

David's cry is a prayer of the heart—one that any of us who have suffered a moral earthquake can readily identify with. The fact is, while we can't lose our salvation, we can certainly lose our joy. And in the face of a moral earthquake, we inevitably do. David did; therefore, he cries out to God for relief. In so doing, he provides a model for us to do likewise. We need not end our lives in despair. We can recover the great joy of our salvation and find our support in the gracious and generous trusses of the Spirit.

JOY

David does not ask for God to restore his salvation. Believers are eternally secure in Him. But even though we can't lose our salvation, we certainly can lose the joy of our salvation.

How would you rate your level of joy?
❑ **Low** ❑ **Medium** ❑ **High**

What contributes to feeling this way?

_____

David prays this great prayer of repentance and confession in Psalm 51 because he has gotten his life out of order. He has put himself first in his life. As a result, he has done something very selfish. So now he prays for the joy of God's salvation to be restored to him.

King David takes his depression to God. He knows it was caused by sin, and he admits as much. Some people never have their joy restored, even though they spend a fortune, going to counselors and reading every book they can read. We live in a world where it seems that our troubles are always someone else's fault; someone else is always to blame. Very few people want to take personal responsibility for their foolish actions, for their deliberate transgressions, for their blatant sins, or for their brazen iniquities. But David does not even hesitate. He knows the truth of his own heart. He knows that his troubles are all his fault. He understands the fact that his moral earthquake was set off by secret moral faults that lay hidden beneath the surface of his seemingly very successful life. Thus he confesses to the Lord, "Against You, You only, have I sinned" (Ps. 51:4).

But now David asks God to let him know the peace and rest that he once enjoyed. Joy is one of the real characteristics of a Christian. However, when we indulge in sin, we jeopardize that joy. Sin and rebellion inevitably cost us the inheritance of joy that is ours in Christ. A Christian may lose the joy of his salvation without losing his salvation. The joy had left King David because he had sinned and because he had tried for a period of several months to cover over that sin.

> **How do you typically react when confronted with your sin?**
> ❏ **Dodge responsibility**
> ❏ **Justify my actions**
> ❏ **Admit responsibility**
> ❏ **Other:** _____

The same thing happens to each of us when we fall into the clutches of temptation and sin. Those of us who know Christ as our personal Savior, who nevertheless live in sin, will most assuredly lose the joy of salvation. To try to cover up our transgressions, iniquities, and sins—to minimize them, to excuse them, or to justify them—will undoubtedly lead to heartsickness, sorrow, and sadness. Perpetuating sin only leads to a loss of the joy of God's gracious and glorious work of salvation.

So, how can the process be reversed? How does the restoration of joy take place? In a word—*grace.* This amazing notion is illustrated all throughout David's great prayer of repentance and confession. The new heart David needed to receive joy could only come from God. The cleansing, the purging, the blotting, and the hearkening that needed to take place in his life could only be accomplished by the sovereign work of God's gracious hand.

> **Use the space in the margin to write a one-sentence description of *grace.***

Notice precisely what it is that David asks for. He says, "Restore to me the joy of Your salvation." It's God's joy, it's God's salvation that is at issue here, not David's joy, not David's salvation. All the attention is on God, not on the poor helpless sinner. The focus is shifted to the One who can make a difference, the One who can make all the difference. No one but God can give us the kind of joy David seeks.

SUSTENANCE

In addition to the restoration of God's great joy, David asks for the sustenance of God's hand and His Spirit. He prays: "And uphold me by Your generous Spirit" (Ps. 51:12).

King David realizes that his only hope is for God to keep him, for God to uphold him. He cannot do it on his own. He wants never again to fall into that situation, so he tells God he will depend solely and completely on Him. He asks God to uphold him by His generous Spirit. The word translated "uphold" is an architectural term for a pillar or column.

David is asking God, "Uphold me, just like a father would uphold his child when teaching him to walk"—not just letting the child grab his father's fingers so he has to hold on, but reaching down and grabbing the child by the wrist so that when he stumbles, his father holds him up along the way.

Describe in the margin a time when you experienced God's upholding touch.

Notorious Repentance and the Fruit of Forgiveness

When is a man usable? When his repentance is as notorious as his sin. The prophet Nathan boldly confronted David in the spirit of grace and truth. Almost immediately, David's heart was broken. His eyes were opened. And, after a year of sinful rebellion, David suddenly turned in humble repentance. He fell on his knees and began to pray a prayer that was subsequently recorded for all posterity—the prayer of repentance and confession we find in Psalm 51.

When do you feel most "usable"? _____

Why? _____

David's repentance was notorious, as notorious as his sin. As a result, God was able to use him again.

Some people try to make deals with God. They say, "God create in me a clean heart and don't cast me away. Restore the joy of Your salvation to me. If You do all that, then I'll teach transgressors; I'll sing Your praises and my tongue shall sing aloud of Your business; my mouth shall show forth Your praise." David was not making a deal with God here. Instead, he simply said, "Not until I'm washed clean, not until I have a new heart and a steadfast spirit within me, not until I've been restored unto the joy of Your salvation, not until then will I be able to do what I want to do: teach transgressors Your ways, letting my mouth and my lips sing forth Your praises and Your righteousness." There is no deal here. There is simply an acknowledgment of what grace produces in a life fully yielded to God's good providence.

How often are you a "deal-maker" with God?
❏ **Never**   ❏ **Often**   ❏ **Occasionally**

What happens when one finds the forgiveness of God? David's great prayer portrays not only our dire need of grace and mercy, but the happy result of grace and mercy in our lives.

In the first half of the prayer, David pours out his heart: "Wash me," he says. "Blot out my transgressions. Cleanse me. I acknowledge my wickedness. My sin is ever before me. I was brought forth in iniquity. Wash me and I'll be whiter than snow. Hide Your face from my sins. Create in me a clean heart." Over and over and over David issues forth a constant cry for God to forgive him of his sin. He uncovers himself so that God can cover him. But the second half of the prayer portrays a threefold commitment to a new life of dedication, a fresh hunger to undertake three essential discipleship tasks: education, exaltation, and exhortation.

Where in your life, right now, do you need to experience forgiveness? _____

What is a practical step that you can make today to move in the direction of forgiveness? _____

Education

When we've come clean before God and have received cleansing, one of the results is that we begin to live a life dedicated to education. David says, "Then I will teach transgressors Your ways" (Ps. 51:13).

There is nothing more dynamic about someone who has just tasted the forgiveness of God than the desire to tell others. One of the reasons Simon Peter was such an effective preacher at Pentecost was that it was just a few days after he had tasted the forgiveness of God. It was fresh to him, so he spoke, preached, and taught with a greater sense of urgency and unction, because of his experience. He had just tasted the forgiveness of God. He knew what it was to be forgiven.

What word would you use to describe your own experience with forgiveness? _____**Why?**

_____

One of the problems in churches today, in Sunday school classes and in pulpits, is that it's been too long since people who are teaching the Word of God have tasted the forgiveness of God themselves. If we are to be effective in our testimony, in our witness, in our education, and in our proclamation, then we are going to have to regularly revisit the well of forgiveness. We are going to have to know the fresh touch of God's grace and mercy.

The fact is, only the forgiven person is fit to teach transgressors the way of the Lord. David knows about what he's going to be teaching. One cannot teach what he does not know. Someone who is computer illiterate cannot teach a class on computer skills. A tour guide can't lead a group of people on a pilgrimage to the Holy Land if he has never been there before—if he has not seen it, not known about it, and not studied about it. He certainly should not be leading, because he just may lead others astray. There is nothing more frightening than to see the blind leading the blind.

King David had been taught in a school of experience. The best teachers are those who teach from personal experience, so David says, "Then I will teach."

Who will David teach? He answers, "Then I will teach transgressors." Look at David's audience. David's heart is heavy for transgressors. That's his target audience. That's who he's interested in teaching. If he couldn't edify the saints, he could certainly teach the sinners. He would be speaking from personal experience to people who were caught in the death throes of sin, just like he once was.

In some churches people have gathered in their own groups for so long that they can hardly remember a time when someone came to grace afresh. In some churches, it has been so long since anyone has been newly converted and has been forgiven that the congregation has all but forgotten about the power of the gospel. For some believers, it has been so long since they have tasted the forgiveness of God themselves that there's little dynamic in their witness, their teaching, or their preaching.

It's a great help when counseling a person, to be able to say, "I know what you're going through. I've been there." There's nothing like personal experience. David said, "Then I'll teach transgressors." He openly—even notoriously—acknowledged his transgressions. Who better to teach transgressors but a forgiven transgressor. There's just something about someone who's been there. There's nothing like personal experience.

Who specifically has helped you as a result of his or her own experience or struggle with sin? _____

Who have you helped as a result of your own struggles? _____

But what would David propose to teach these transgressors? He says, "Then I will teach transgressors Your ways." The ways of God. That Hebrew word literally means "your road," "your path," "your journey." David will offer the lost a map. He will provide them with emergency road service. And the result of this teaching? He says, "Sinners shall be converted to You." Once they know the way, those transgressors will return to God.

What is the result of finding the forgiveness of God? It has been a long time since many of us have tasted it. We have harbored resentments and never asked God to forgive us. We have had broken fellowship with other believers in Christ and never asked God to forgive us. But once we do ask for forgiveness, what is the result? We'll have a life dedicated to teaching transgressors, to using our own life experiences for good. We will have the providential opportunity to use our moral earthquakes as a part of our testimony for God's glory. We will be able to take the tragic circumstances of our failures and use them to minister to others. To what end? So that folks might know God's way. And, ultimately, so that sinners might be converted to Him.

Exaltation

The fruit of forgiveness also includes a new dedication to exaltation. Thus David prays: "Deliver me from the guilt of bloodshed, O God, the God of my salvation, and my tongue shall sing aloud of Your righteousness. O Lord, open my lips, and my mouth shall show forth Your praise" (Ps. 51:14–15).

King David says, "If God forgave me—and He did—then I will surely sing and I will praise His name." I will praise. That word literally means "a song" or "a hymn of praise." Only the man or woman who knows the forgiveness of God has a song in his or her heart. Those who don't know the forgiveness of God just go through the motions. They may come into corporate worship, mouth some words, and make some noise, but they don't sing from their hearts.

David's lips had been sealed for a year. He was in a barren foreign land of the soul. He was wandering in the parched desert land of Nod. The children of Israel, when down in Babylon, asked, "How can we sing the Lord's song in a foreign land?" and they hung their harps on the willow trees.

There are a lot of folks like that. David couldn't sing for all those months. He had no song. He refused to admit that he had done anything wrong. His lips had been sealed by shame. He knew that if he sang praises to the Lord, those in that inner circle who really knew would know what a hypocrite he actually was. But after his prayer of confession and repentance, a song began to well up in his heart. His first reaction, after wanting to teach others, was to sing praises to God. This had once been his very life. From the shepherd's fields outside Bethlehem to the anguished royal courts of King Saul, he would take his harp and sing songs of praise. This was the heart of the legacy he ultimately left, exemplified in the psalms. No one knew the songs of praise more than David.

What things take away your desire to praise God?

_____

Notice that David says he will sing of the righteousness of God. One would expect him to sing of God's mercy; but no, he says he will sing of God's righteousness. He realized that God's mercy was only possible through the righteous demands of the law being met.

So, what happens to a person when he finds the forgiveness of God? First he wants to teach transgressors God's ways. Then his life becomes a testimony and sacrifice of praise. And where does that lead? It leads to a life dedicated to exhortation.

How often is your worship a response to God's forgiveness? ❑ Never   ❑ Often   ❑ Occasionally

day Five

Exhortation

The final fruit of forgiveness takes the form of an exhortation. The sacrifice King David had to bring before the Lord was a broken and a crushed spirit. This is indeed an exhortation to us.

What does the Lord desire from us? Our sacrifices? Our service? No, He wants us—a broken heart and a broken and contrite spirit. He doesn't want gifts. He wants the giver.

What do you think it means to have "a broken heart and a broken and contrite spirit"?

_____

_____

David closes his great prayer of confession and repentance, saying: "Do good in Your good pleasure to Zion. Build the walls of Jerusalem. Then You shall be pleased with the sacrifices of righteousness, with burnt offering and whole burnt offering; then they shall offer bulls on Your altar" (Ps. 51:18–19).

One might say, "Hmmm, is that a contradiction? Didn't David just say, God didn't want sacrifices?"

Indeed, David asserts, "You do not delight in burnt offerings, or else I'd give it to you." But there is no contradiction at all. What King David asked for Jerusalem, we should ask for the church. What God did for King David, God will do for any and all of us—forgive us, make us healthy spiritually, and make us happy and whole.

When we get right with God, our energy and our prayers move past our own selfish interests and are directed to the entire family of faith. And when we are cleansed and restored with the joy of salvation, that will be our prayer, "Do good to Zion, by your own good pleasure." It will be our greatest pleasure to edify the body of Christ.

The fact is, it is more important what you are when you pray than it is what you pray. And thus, the greatest of the fruits of forgiveness is the fact that God makes us anew. He makes us new creations. He enables us to be what we are supposed to be, so that we can, in turn, do what we are supposed to do.

In what specific ways has God made you anew?

_____

_____

To the Leader:

Before the Session

1. Consider a quick overview of David's story as presented in 1 and 2 Samuel. Be ready to give a brief overview of David's life, personality, and struggles. Use a Bible dictionary to help you in this preparation.

2. Dealing with the subjects referenced in this lesson is tough. It's likely that some of your learners have been touched by depression, relational conflict, spiritual confusion, and so forth. Be sensitive to the needs of your class. If possible, find out about counseling resources your church or community offers to a person or couple struggling with the subject matter discussed in this lesson. Your pastor should have information on resources available.

3. Have available large tear sheets, markers, and tape or tacks.

During the Session

1. As a class, investigate the life of David as presented in 2 Samuel 11:1–12:25 and in Psalm 51. This is a lot of Scripture content. If the class is large enough, break into smaller groups and give out Scripture assignments. Allow each group to read a portion of the assigned Scripture and then report to the class about what they read.

2. Ask: *How would you describe David's level of joy?* Ask learners to share how they responded to the second interactive activity in Day 1. Refer to the third paragraph under the "Joy" section on page 134: "King David takes his depression to God." Have someone read aloud this paragraph. Ask: *Do you agree or disagree with Dr. Hawkins's conclusion that we try to blame something or someone else for our own depression?* Make sure to emphasize that many people deal with depression and require special care from a professional. Going to God is the most important thing we can do, but sometimes God uses counselors and physicians to help us deal with deep-seated depression.

3. Ask learners to share how they typically react when confronted with their sin (refer to the third interactive activity in Day 1). Ask: *How does grace play a crucial role in our dealing with sin and guilt?*

Many of us know, at least in theory, that God will forgive us when we sin. Yet we live our lives with guilt and regret. *What does it look like to be "restored"? Does it mean that I forget about my sin? Does God forget about my sin? How do I rediscover joy in my faith and in life in general after I have sinned?* These questions haunt many who call themselves followers of Jesus. This lesson offers practical help for those who long to find joy once again. King David's process of restoration after his sin and loss of joy is the basis for this study.

4. Ask learners to share how they responded to the first interactive activity in Day 2. Dr. Hawkins emphasized that David became most usable before God when he repented. Ask learners to identify within Psalm 51 how this is apparent. Explain that we often try to get around "coming clean." Or we try to make deals with God. Ask learners to share how they responded to the second interactive activity in Day 2.

5. Ask learners to summarize what Dr. Hawkins meant when he spoke of "Education" in Day 3. Lead learners to use Psalm 51 to justify their response. Follow up by asking learners to share how learning from others who have made mistakes has had an impact on them. Challenge learners to become "teachers of transgressors" based on their own experiences with sin and forgiveness. Utilize the second interactive activity in Day 3 to facilitate this discussion.

6. Ask: *How did praising God play a role in David's journey of restoration? Why was this important?* Ask learners to offer their responses to the second interactive activity in Day 4.

7. Refer to the first interactive activity on Day 5. Emphasize to learners that spiritual brokenness ironically can lead to great joy and relief. When we acknowledge our sinfulness, we find the arms of a grace-ful and forgiving God. Ask learners to describe the way God restores us. Utilize the second interactive activity in Day 5 to emphasize how God makes us anew.

8. Using a large sheet of paper, write on the top of the page the words *Restoring Joy*. Under this title allow learners to list lessons learned from this discussion and particularly from David's experience with God's forgiveness. Then, using a different colored marker, ask learners to come up with one "take-away" application that this lesson teaches about how to protect one's self from a moral earthquake. After completing this exercise, post the paper on the wall with those from the former lessons to remind learners what they are learning.

Rescue Efforts

day One

The Ministry of Restoration

If a person suffers a moral earthquake, if he crumbles under the pressures of temptation, if his faults cause his downfall, what are we to do? Especially if this person is a Christian brother or sister, how are we to react? What is our role? Indeed, are we to do anything?

It's not a particularly comfortable subject for any of us to discuss, but we simply must talk about the subject of picking up the pieces of broken lives—the ministry of restoration. Certainly, it is not a subject the Bible avoids. For instance, the apostle Paul forthrightly asserts: "Brethren, if a man is overtaken in any trespass, you who are spiritual restore such a one in a spirit of gentleness, considering yourself lest you also be tempted. Bear one another's burdens, and so fulfill the law of Christ" (Gal. 6:1–2).

This may well be one of the most important lessons of all in the realm of temptation for the church of Jesus Christ: What do we do when someone falls and falters? We, the members of the body of Christ, must restore that brother or sister.

In your own observation, what has happened when someone has fallen into sin or faltered?

Now what do you think would happen if a church began to be known as a place of true restoration? If it became a place where those who are down could get up, a place where those who are out could get back in, not a place of condemnation but of confirmation, a place of new beginnings? I will tell you what would happen: Men and women from all over—men and women with wounded hearts and hopes—would flock to such a church to find hope and to find healing. This is the church we find in the New Testament.

Sadly, many Christians are not active in the ministry of restoration. More sadly still, not many churches are involved in the ministry of restoration. In the body of Christ we have a responsibility to one another. Paul tells us that the responsibility we have to one another is threefold. We should hunt him up, help him up, and hold him up.

day Two

Hunting, Helping, and Holding

"Brethren, if any man is overcome in a trespass, you who are spiritual hunt him up." Go to him, restore him, take the initiative. Most of us wait for our wounded, fallen friends to come crawling back, saying, "I'm sorry." But so often, the guilt and the shame that comes in being overcome by temptation prevent one from doing that very thing. In fact, a lot of people are not in church today simply because they're afraid of rejection. They've been overtaken in a trespass, and the fear is that if they should come back to church, they would be rejected!

The ministry of restoration, to the believer, involves hunting him up—seeking him out. We have to go to him; he won't come to us.

Who do you know who needs to be sought after?

_____

Secondly, we are to help him up. Paul says, "Restore him." Our responsibility does not end in seeking out our fallen friends but in restoring them. And then that's not enough. We're not to stop there. We are to hold them up. Paul admonishes us, "Bear one another's burdens and so fulfill the law of Christ." And the law of Christ is the law of love.

Why don't we typically choose to bear others' burdens?

_____

Now what do we do when we find a fallen friend? When dealing with temptation, it's not enough just to talk about everything that precedes the fall, yet sometimes that's what we do in the church of Jesus Christ. We're good about how to overcome temptation, how to spot it, how to stop it, but what do we do when someone falls? We are to hunt them up. By and large, in our generation, we have not been very good at this.

We're better at writing him off and then saying to one another, "I told you so." We like to wait for that fallen one to come back to us, but the Scripture is explicit. It says that our position is to hunt him up, to be the initiator, and to go to him. Don't wait for him to hunt you up for help. It's not going to happen. Many of us with good intentions have seen friends, overtaken in trespass, in sin, and have just been waiting for them to come back, just been waiting for them to repent, to be restored, to come back—perhaps crawling—to us. It's not going to happen.

Why? Many will not return because of guilt—the shame that sin brings; for others, it's the fear of rejection. We are to take the initiative.

What holds people you know from coming back to church?

_____

Now the issue: this is a family matter. This isn't talking about going to the lost. Paul issues this admonition to the "brethren." The Greek word literally means "of the same womb." Paul is directing us to take proactive measures to protect our fellow family of faith members, those who may have succumbed to temptation and to sin.

When are we to engage in this ministry of restoration? Paul says, "If a man is overtaken in any trespass." That word "overtaken" is very interesting in the Greek. It literally means "caught in the act." It conveys a certain element of surprise. If a man is overtaken—to his surprise—in a trespass, then we are to restore him.

So here is a person who is caught, and he falls. Those little secret faults have been running through his life. He didn't think there was anything to them; he thought he was all right; he thought he'd get away with it. Now, all of a sudden, a moral earthquake has struck.

Paul says if a brother has been overtaken in a trespass in this way, then there is something for us to do. We are to hunt him up and seek to restore him. He could get hurt if he stays out there, outside the boundary lines of God's Word. All of us are susceptible to being overcome by trespasses, even the great men of faith in the Bible: Moses, Elijah, and David.

One day, David stepped over the line, trespassed outside the boundary lines of the Word of God. Yet he was fortunate enough to have a friend named Nathan who hunted him up, helped him up, held him up, confronted him in a spirit of gentleness, and said, "You're that man." We read Psalm 51 and see the repentant heart of David, how that friend of his helped him and held him up.

Paul wrote the Galatian epistle at the end of his first missionary journey. Remember what happened on that first missionary journey? There was a young man by the name of John Mark. He accompanied Paul and Barnabas and then went AWOL. He quit. He gave up. He left them in the lurch and went back home.

How was John Mark restored? Barnabas was his friend, and what did Barnabas do? He hunted John Mark up. Being a spiritual man, he hunted Mark up and helped him up; he restored him. Then he held him up, he stood by him, and he encouraged him. John Mark went on to leave us that Gospel that bears his name—the Gospel of Mark.

Why? Because Mark had a friend who—when he got outside the boundary lines and was overtaken in a trespass—sought him out and restored him. Barnabas didn't wait for John Mark to come crawling back, saying, "I'm sorry." He went out and, in a spirit of gentleness, hunted him up, helped him up, held him up, and God gave him another opportunity.

What is one specific way you can seek to restore someone you know who feels estranged from church and God?

_____

day Three

The Role of the Spiritual

Not everyone in the church of Jesus Christ is supposed to be involved in the ministry of restoration. Paul says the initiator in this ministry of restoration must be uniquely qualified: "You who are spiritual." The reason is simple: Carnal people, those who are not spiritual, will do more damage than they will help.

The call is issued to "you who are spiritual," not you who are holier-than-thou. This is not open season for church people to think it's their God-given call to go out to everybody overtaken in a trespass and confront them, seeking to be part of the ministry of restoration. It is only for those who are spiritual, not self-righteous, not holier-than-thou.

The Greek word for "spiritual" here literally means "one who is filled with and governed by the Holy Spirit." The call to restoration is not to be heeded by everyone. Only those who are spiritual need apply for this job.

Earlier in his Galatian letter Paul defined just who "the spiritual" were. They were those whose lives genuinely evidence the fruit of the Spirit.

Read what Paul wrote in Galatians 5:22–6:1, printed in the margin. What in this passage catches your attention with regard to restoring someone who struggles with sin?

_____

The one who is spiritual reacts with genuine concern and genuine remorse. He is aware that if this is a true brother who is wounded, he's wounded too. They're members of the same family. They are parts of the same body, and if a part of his body is hurting, he's hurting too. Those who are spiritual realize that. The church must get past the false assumption that the one who has fallen is the one who needs to be the initiator of restoration.

"The fruit of the Spirit is love, joy, peace, longsuffering, kindness, goodness, faithfulness, gentleness, self-control. Against such there is no law. And those who are Christ's have crucified the flesh with its passions and desires. If we live in the Spirit, let us also walk in the Spirit. Let us not become conceited, provoking one another, envying one another. Brethren, if a man is overtaken in a trespass, you who are spiritual restore such a one" (Gal. 5:22–6:1).

And what are spiritual believers to do? Pursuit—even loving pursuit—of our fallen brother is not enough. We must take the process of restoration to the next step.

The word for "restore" literally means "to mend something that is broken or that is torn." It is used in the Gospels to describe nets that were in need of repair. It is also used to describe a broken bone, one in need of mending. The word picture portrays the idea of putting a bone back in place so that it mends and is useful again or fixing rends in a net so that it can be used to fish again.

In the ministry of reconciliation and restoration, God uses those who are spiritual to mend that which is torn and to heal that which is broken. He wants to use us, those of us who are spiritual. He wants to use us as His orthopedic physicians to set the broken bones of our time in place so that He can do His own work of healing. He wants to use us to do that, those of us whose lives are characterized by love, joy, peace, gentleness, faithfulness, and self-control. God wants us to be His fixer-uppers.

Is it easy or difficult to perceive yourself as a "spiritual person"? Why?

_____

What makes you hesitant to serve as a spiritual person capable of restoring someone?

_____

How do your hesitations match up with Galatians 5:22—6:1?

_____

Here is a man, and the secret faults in his life have erupted into a moral earthquake. Instead of talking about him or lamenting the fact that it's done, we are to go to him, restore him, help him to set those things in place in a spirit of gentleness, so that God can bring hope and healing.

The sad commentary with a lot of believers today is that instead of going to a broken brother, they go to others and talk about him.

I Spy

Some like to criticize, some like to condemn, some like to castigate, others like to critique, and some like to cancel—just forget the offending parties. Some say, "It's none of my business. He made his bed; let him lie in it!" But the Bible says, "Brethren, if a man is overtaken in a trespass, you who are spiritual, put that bone in place, mend that torn net."

George W. Truett once said, "I think nothing of that system of espionage which is forever spying out people to catch up with their weaknesses and their faults."

Some churches are into spy activities. There is no place in the church of Jesus Christ for brothers and sisters lying in wait, spying on one another in a spirit of espionage to bring down instead of to build up, to tear down instead of holding up. Our business is to restore. Too many times the very place that God has ordained to be the center of restoration—the church of Jesus Christ—has become the center of condemnation. That's why so many churches are empty today. Instead of being the very center of the place of restoration where wounded broken lives can come, be set together, and become whole, they become places of condemnation.

How would you grade your church community as far as being a place of restoration? (Circle your response.)

A+   A   B+   B   C+   C   D   F

Why did you select this particular grade? _____

_____

God uses us as His agents of restoration. We're to help up those who have fallen.

Imagine going out during the noon hour in a metropolitan area when the streets are filled with people—pedestrians walking everywhere—and seeing a lady step off of a curb. She trips and breaks her arm. Lying there in the street, she is writhing in pain.

One person walks by and says to his friend, "Look at her lying there. She's broken her arm." Another sees her lying there in pain and simply criticizes her, "You're in the way of pedestrian traffic. We're trying to get by here, and we have to step over you. Can't you move?" Someone else stops, but only to counsel the woman. "You know, if you had watched where you were going you wouldn't have tripped over that curb." Now she really needs to hear that, doesn't she? Someone else looks on from a distance and condemns the poor woman. "That's stupid. That is so stupid. She shouldn't have done that."

Sound ridiculous? Certainly it does! And yet that is precisely how we act when we find that a brother or a sister has been caught in a trespass.

Just because that lady has broken her arm does not mean it must be amputated. It can be mended. It can be put back in place. It can be restored, and it can become useful again.

Why is the church of Jesus Christ hobbling through this world, limping and struggling along in many places? Because there are a lot of broken bones in the body of Christ that have never been properly set. The thrust of the word *restore* is in getting the wrongdoer back to where he should be. It is in getting the bones back in place so they can be mended and become useful again. It is in getting the nets mended so they can be useful again. It is in getting fallen Christians restored to usefulness, just as strong as ever.

I wonder how many broken bones there are in the body of Christ today? How many wounded lives are there? If a broken bone is not set properly, it may never heal the way it should, and the longer it waits to get set, the longer it gets set in it's own way—deformed. If the believer is not restored, the strength of the church is weakened.

We are members of the same family. We are soldiers in the same army. We are bones, as it were, in the same body. We are all a part of the same net, and when there is a tear in the net, it ceases to be effective. When a part of that net is ripped and torn, fish get out.

We need to realize our world is hurting and broken, and, "brethren, if a man is overtaken in a trespass, you who are spiritual restore [him] in a spirit of gentleness, considering yourself, lest you also be tempted. Bear one another's burdens, and so fulfill the law of Christ" (Gal. 6:1–2).

Set those broken bones so they can walk again. Mend those torn nets so they can fish again. Restore those fallen lives so they can live again. That's what we're to do. We're to hunt them up and help them up and hold them up. This vision of a place of restoration, with us acting as agents of restoration, should be the goal of our churches. Only through application of these principles can we hope to restore the aftereffects of a moral earthquake.

How would you grade yourself as an agent of restoration? (Circle your response.)

A+   A   B+   B   C+   C   D   F

Why did you select this particular grade? _____

_____

day Five

The Process of Restoration

In the aftermath of a great natural disaster such as an earthquake, a tremendous amount of labor must be exerted. Things cannot simply be left alone. The devastation and destruction cannot be ignored. The mess won't go away if we simply ignore it long enough.

So, everyone has to pitch in, work together, and labor side by side. The entire community must be mobilized. Otherwise the work will never get done, and life will never get back to anything resembling normalcy.

Similarly, the clean-up effort following a moral earthquake can be an enormous undertaking. Yet however difficult, however unpleasant, and however unnerving, it must be done. And it must be done in cooperation with others. It requires a group effort. The entire community of faith must be mobilized.

It's always a good habit in Bible study to ask ourselves several questions: *When? Who? What? How?* and *Why?* When we do this, it is utterly amazing how beautifully and clearly Scripture unfolds for us.

So in Galatians 6:1–2 we ask: When? The answer: When one is overtaken in a trespass. Who? You who are spiritual. What? Restore him. How? In a spirit of gentleness. Why? Considering yourself, lest you also be tempted.

Why is recognizing your own vulnerability important?

_____

By asking those simple questions, a wealth of truth emerges from this passage of God's Word. We are to hunt up those who have fallen. We are to simultaneously help them up. And we are to do it all in a spirit of gentleness, meekness, and humility—remembering from whence we have come.

The word translated "gentleness" in the Greek text was literally used of "an animal that has been completely tamed—domesticated." It describes a wild stallion that some cowboy has broken. It's no longer wild. It no longer bucks. The cowboy can get on the back of that horse, flick the reigns a little bit to the left, and the horse, will turn to the left; a little to the right and it'll turn right. He can pull back slightly and it'll stop. That wild stallion has come under the control of his master. That is the word picture that the Apostle Paul uses to describe the kind of spirit we are to display in the process of restoration: it is a spirit of *gentleness*.

And why should spiritual believers act toward those who have suffered a moral earthquake in this manner? Paul tells us, "Considering yourself, lest you also be tempted." Being spiritual doesn't guarantee that you will never suffer a moral earthquake yourself. As the Apostle Paul elsewhere warned believers, "If you think you are standing firm, be careful that you don't fall" (1 Cor. 10:12).

How have your efforts to spiritually help others affected your own spiritual well-being?

_____

Before the Session

1. Galatians 5:22–6:2 is the Focal Passage for this lesson. Before class read through Paul's entire Letter to the Galatians. Be ready to give necessary background to your class about Paul's reason for writing this letter. You may wish to consult the *Illustrated Holman Bible Dictionary*, which is available in both printed form and as an online resource (visit resources at *www.Lifeway.com* to access this dictionary).

2. Be prepared to help learners understand how we interpret the word *restore*. Find a piece of solid wood furniture in your house that is worn and scratched. If it is small enough, bring this piece of furniture to class. If not, take a picture of it to class.

3. Bring three-by-five-inch index cards to class. These will be used as part of an application exercise.

4. Bring a large tear sheet to class along with colored markers.

During the Session

1. Invite learners to share how they responded to the interactive exercise in Day 1. Read Galatians 6:1-2. Ask learners to describe what they think the word *restore* means. Either display the worn piece of furniture or show the picture. Ask: *What does it mean to restore a piece of furniture?* Follow up by asking: *How is the process of restoring furniture similar to our process of spiritual restoration?*

2. Ask: *Would you describe yourself as someone who was pursued or "hunted," as Dr. Hawkins described in the reading for Day 2?* Encourage learners to share how other Christians have pursued them when they have fallen into sin. Direct learners to consider how they intentionally seek to restore others who have sinned. To facilitate discussion, refer to the second interactive exercise in Day 2. Encourage learners to brainstorm ways they can actively live out Galatians 6:2 (bearing burdens). Draw on their responses to the fourth interactive exercise in Day 2.

3. Ask: *How would you describe someone who is spiritual?* [Learners can find a definition in the third paragraph of Day 3.] Ask: *Do you see yourself as spiritual? Why or why not?* Emphasize that the Holy Spirit makes

To the Leader:

Restoration is not an individual pursuit; it is a community event. First, as last week's lessons emphasized, restoration is an event that involves God. Second, the church community is an integral part of the process of restoration. Challenge learners to consider who they specifically can reach out to over the next few weeks with a message of restoration.

believers spiritual. State that God has designed for mature believers to assist in restoring those who have fallen into sin. For additional discussion, refer to the second interactive exercise in Day 3.

4. Allow learners time to share their responses to the two interactive activities in Day 4. Allow enough time for discussion as to why learners feel the way they do. Make sure to guard the discussion. Don't let people drift toward bad-mouthing the church. Instead, facilitate a constructive critique of how the church serves to restore people. Then direct learners to consider their role(s) in restoration.

5. Ask: *How should we understand a "spirit of gentleness" as described in Galatians 6:1-2?* Refer to discussion of this concept in Day 5. Emphasize that gentleness is easier when we realize our own vulnerability to sin. Regarding vulnerability, ask learners how they responded to the first interactive of Day 5. Have learners read aloud together 1 Corinthians 10:12 to emphasize our spiritual vulnerability.

6. For the purpose of application, pass out three-by-five-inch index cards—one per person. Ask learners to write the name of at least one person they know who needs to experience restoration. Challenge learners to keep this card with them. Tell them that when they look at the card, they should pray for the person(s) listed. As they pray, they also should make a plan as to how they will help this person experience the gentleness of God's forgiveness and restoration.

7. Using a large sheet of paper, write on the top of the page the words *Rescue Efforts*. Under this title allow learners to list lessons learned from this discussion and from Galatians 5:22–6:2. Then, using a different colored marker, ask learners to come up with one "take-away" application that this lesson teaches about how to protect one's self from a moral earthquake. After completing this exercise, post the paper on the wall with those from the former lessons to remind learners what they are learning.

Quake Proofing

How Can We Keep Pure?

Early in 1995 an earthquake measuring 7.5 on the Richter scale struck the oil town of Neftegorsk on the island of Sakhalin, off the Pacific coast of Russia. Blocks of five-story apartment buildings collapsed, crushing hundreds of people. Of the three thousand people who lived in the town, about two thousand were killed.

Shoddy Soviet engineering contributed to the destruction. Although earthquakes are common in the region, the buildings in Neftegorsk were not built to withstand earthquakes. Because budget cuts had closed five of the island's six seismic stations, the city received no early warning. "We live from earthquake to earthquake," said Aleksei Nikolayev, director of the Center for Seismology and Engineering in Moscow. "Until something happens, no one does anything about it."

Today we can do a great deal to prepare for these geologic disruptions. We know how to build buildings that can withstand earthquakes. We have instruments that can detect signs of an approaching quake. But Neftegorsk did not use this knowledge. The city failed to prepare, and when the earthquake hit, the city was caught off guard.

In the same way that communities can prepare for the cataclysm of earthquakes, we can prepare for the catastrophe of moral earthquakes. We can build upon sturdy foundations—solid enough to withstand the worst disturbances imaginable. We can ensure the safety of those around us. We can quake-proof our lives simply by following the prescriptives of wise living outlined in the Scriptures.

The psalmist posed the question, "How can a young man keep his way pure?" (Ps. 119:9, NASB). At first blush, we might answer rather negatively. After all, we live in the midst of a culture that is literally wracked with seismic disturbances of monumental proportions.

More than one million teenagers will run away from home this year in America, many of them because of physical or sexual abuse in the home. One out of every ten teenage girls will get pregnant this year. Half of all marriages will end in divorce, leaving hundreds of thousands of teenagers fearful of making commitments themselves later in life. And before the year is through, half a million teenagers will attempt suicide.

The present generation faces an entirely different culture than the one in which their parents were raised. Our teenagers today are involved in a culture that constantly is dragging them down into a moral abyss. Young people beginning careers today are facing pressures they have never known before. Others are leaving home for the first time, going off to college. They will be faced with increasing challenges: no one to check on them, living in coeducational dorms, no curfews, roommates—some with very different moral values—and all sorts of things taking place in the halls of their dormitories. Other teenagers are entering high school or junior high for the first time. They will be faced with increasing pressures of wanting to be accepted, wanting to find their place, and trying to fit in with a world that has gone mad. And it's not just the young people. The rest of us too are bombarded by antibiblical messages and values all the time from all sides. In fact, we who have been on the way a long time have become desensitized to just how far our culture has subtly changed our thinking, our values, and our morals.

What social/moral issues seem to be at the forefront in your community?

So the question the psalmist poses is as startlingly relevant today as when it was first penned, "How can we keep pure?" And the answer to that question is certainly no less urgent today than it was then.

Five Big "I"s, part 1

The first word of the question *how* is typical of youth—as well as the rest of us. It is a good question. How can I survive adolescence? How can I make it through these college years and stay pure in morals, pure in mind, and pure in my motives? How can I make it through this transitional change into this career while surrounded by temptations I never really knew existed? How can I make it through these teenage years when my body keeps changing, and I feel so dumb and insecure and hurt? How can I live different from my colleagues who say and do that which goes against my commitment to Christ? How?

In the midst of all, God's Word speaks poignantly. The psalmist gave us the answer.

Read the psalmist's answer, printed in the margin. How, according to Psalm 119:10-16, can we live differently in a world of moral fallout?

_____

Young people, young adults, and all of us are engaged in the most promiscuous culture known to the Western world, right here in America. Several factors come into play. The first is an element of *intimidation*. We have raised a generation in a public education system that has intimidated our young people intellectually into a belief in relativism—into accepting the absurd notion that everything is relative, that there are no moral absolutes. This intellectually indefensible position has given rise to all sorts of things, such as coeducational dorms. A preacher and his wife were sending their daughter to a school in the East. When they took her there to check into the dorm, they discovered it was coeducational. However, there was one floor that was reserved for only girls. Relieved, they were going to place her there until the dorm mother said,

"With my whole heart I have sought You; Oh, let me not wander from Your commandments! Your word have I hidden in my heart, that I might not sin against You. Blessed are you, O LORD! Teach me Your statutes. With my lips I have declared all the judgments of Your mouth. I have rejoiced in the way of Your testimonies, as much as in all riches. I will meditate on Your precepts, and contemplate on Your ways. I will delight myself in Your statutes; I will not forget Your word" (Ps. 119:10–16).

159

"Unless she's a lesbian, she doesn't want to be on this floor, because this floor is made up of lesbians." So she moved to a coeducational floor.

On a scale of 1 to 10 (1 being never and 10 being very often), how often does *relativism* show up in the following relationships?

Family: ____ Work: ____ Friends: ____ Church: ____

This is the way it is in many college campuses around America. There are few moral absolutes anymore. How can we keep pure in a culture that is telling our young people that no one can stay pure? It teaches them sex education from the time they are knee high, speaks very little—if any—about abstinence, and hands out condoms in secondary schools. How can we keep pure in a culture that keeps telling us we can't?

Well, young people can stay pure, and many do. The greatest gift young persons can give to their future husbands or wives is their own moral purity.

Isolation is another problem in today's culture. The urbanization of America, the move to the cities, has brought anonymity and loneliness. You'd think it would be just the opposite, but it is not. No one knows who you are, no one knows where you go, no one knows what you do, no one knows what you watch, and no one cares. You are away from those who care. Many children come home to houses that are empty after school. They sit in front of the television set and watch talk shows that are filled with degradation and blatant sexual talk.

What is one way you can avoid the moral vulnerability that isolation creates?

_____

_____

_____

Five Big "I"s, part 2

Third, there exists a lot of *imitation* role models, especially of families in our culture. They are called "families," but it is really a facade. One example is the "family" of a fourteen-year-old young man named Peter. His parents divorced when he was six years old. He lives with his mom, but spends weekends with his dad. He hates it because his dad's new girlfriend doesn't like him. Time with his mom is strained too. She remarried when he was nine; she had another little boy who is now four, then divorced again. Peter and his little halfbrother get along well, but his halfbrother is gone a lot visiting his dad. Peter's mom married a third time, and her new husband has two teenage kids who push Peter around and treat him badly. His mom and dad fight a lot on the phone—mostly over child support payments. His dad thinks they are too high; Peter says that makes him feel rotten and worthless. He notes that his daddy had money last year to buy a new sports car. He wonders if his dad really loves him because he seems more interested in his new girlfriend. That's Peter's family. The name is the same—*family*—yet it is a hollow corrupted version of the word. It's a counterfeit use of the term.

In one sentence, how would you describe your family experience?

_____

Fourth, there is the element of *information*—false information. The media has a negative influence on moral values. Recently the front page of my hometown newspaper carried a big story on "a new kind of family," about two gay men and two lesbians who wanted to have children through artificial insemination, and they did. Then in the "Metro" section there was another big article on the gay lifestyle and the acceptability of it. Then in the "Today" section of the same paper another article advocated the acceptance of the gay lifestyle. It is overwhelming and morally wrong—yet we are bombarded with it all the time.

Rate how each source of information influences you.

THE MEDIA	❑ **Insignificantly**	❑ **Significantly**
FAMILY	❑ **Insignificantly**	❑ **Significantly**
WORK	❑ **Insignificantly**	❑ **Significantly**
EDUCATION	❑ **Insignificantly**	❑ **Significantly**
CHURCH	❑ **Insignificantly**	❑ **Significantly**

Lastly, there is the element of *inculcation*—impressing something upon the mind through repetitive, frequent repetition. Today we are bombarded by advertising that tells us a hundred times a day that illicit sex is normal, that it ought to be the center of our lives. Consumerism teaches us to find satisfaction and hope in materialism and self-indulgence.

How often do you feel like you are a victim of inculcation? Circle your response.

Never   **Often**

When many of us parents were teenagers, the moral climate was drastically different. We didn't have to deal with intimidation and relativism—the Ten Commandments were on the wall of public school classrooms. There were moral absolutes. We didn't have to deal with isolation. Everyone knew their neighbors. On my block we knew who lived next door to us. We knew almost everybody. In fact, if one kid did something wrong, the neighbors would take care of it, and Dad would thank them for it later.

It's a challenging world out there. So the question is, "How can a young man keep his way pure?"

Know the Word

According to the psalmist, in the midst of all these cultural challenges, we have but one chance—to center our lives in the Word of God. The psalmist says, first of all, to keep the Word of God in your head. Know the Word.

God's Word is a stable rock that we must use to support us. It is our foundation. We can keep ourselves pure. In your head, know the Word. The psalmist wrote: "Blessed are You, O Lord! Teach me Your statutes" (Ps. 119:12). It is difficult for the Bible to impact your life if you know little about it. In school you are taught information and then comes a test. If you don't know the material, you fail the test and eventually the course. The same is true of a football team. Each team member learns all the plays. If a player doesn't know the playbook, he won't know where he's supposed to go when the ball is snapped. He will be out of step, affect the whole team, and lose the game.

It's the same with the Word of God. The most important book in anyone's educational experience is the Bible, but it will do you little good if you don't study it. There are a lot of believers who say they love the Word but never study it, never learn it. How can you keep yourself pure? By saying, "Lord, teach me Your statutes."

What parts of the Bible do you feel most familiar with?

_____

What parts do you feel the least familiar with?

_____

Everytime we study the Bible we ought to pray with the psalmist, "Open my eyes, that I may see wondrous things from Your law"

163

(Ps. 119:18). To fully understand God's Word, we need spiritual help. The Bible is a foreign language without the Holy Spirit's interpretation.

Some young people go to college where professors scoff at what the individual learned in church since nursery days. They are told, even in many so-called Christian colleges, that the first eleven chapters of Genesis are not historical. They are told that, at best, Jonah is an allegory. Yet long after those skeptics are gone, the Word of God will still stand true. As Isaiah proclaimed, "The grass withers, the flower fades, but the word of our God stands forever" (Isa. 40:8).

There will be times when those going off to college may feel lonely, burdened, and rejected. During such times they may be tempted to go out with the wrong crowd and do things they shouldn't. Let those be times when, as the psalmist says, "When I was afflicted, it was good for me, for then I learned Your statutes." Make up your mind that not a day is going to go by in your life that you don't expose your mind to the Word of God. How can a young person—any person—keep himself pure? In your head, know the Word of God.

Describe one way you will implement a steady diet of Bible study into your daily routine.

Stow the Word

Second, the psalmist says to keep God's Word in your heart. Stow the Word in your heart. Hide it there. The psalmist said it well: "Your word I have hidden in my heart, that I might not sin against You" (Ps. 119:11). And again, "I will meditate on Your precepts, and contemplate Your ways" (Ps. 119:15).

It's not enough to keep the Word in your head. You need to store it in your heart—memorize it, then meditate on it. Do you remember the instruction God gave Joshua? "This Book of the Law shall not depart from your mouth, but you shall meditate in it day and night, that you may observe to do all that is written in it. For then you will make your way prosperous, and then you will have good success" (Josh. 1:8).

Some of us are crossing over into a new land, like Joshua. And if that advice is good for those going into Canaan, it is certainly good for those going into college, those going into careers, and for all of us who wish to quake-proof our lives.

Meditate on God's Word. Going over and over the Word deepens its impression. It is like a tune that we can't get out of our minds. Imagine what would happen if we couldn't get Scripture out of our heads. What would be the effect if we memorized Scripture daily? What would our witness be like if we always carried a Scripture memory card in our pocket?

Why not try this: For one month, stow the Word of God in your life. How? Take the Book of Proverbs and read through one chapter each morning. Thirty-one days in the month, thirty-one chapters in Proverbs. Whatever the day is you start reading, you start on that chapter. Keep it correlated with the day of the month, then you'll always know what chapter you're in. It will take five to ten minutes each morning. As you read that chapter, ask God to give you one verse to memorize. Write it down on a card and keep it in your pocket. Then when you're eating breakfast, take it out, read it, and put it back in your pocket. When you're at a stoplight, take it out, read it again, and put it in your pocket again. Do this as often as you can throughout the day. Meditate on it all day long. What will happen if you keep doing this all day with one verse? You will know it by heart. Then the next time temptation beckons, you will be prepared. You will be like the psalmist, who wrote: "Your word I have hidden in my heart, that I might not sin against You" (Ps. 119:11).

Why should we memorize Scripture? The psalmist tells us: "You are my hiding place and my shield; I hope in Your word" (Ps. 119:114). When you memorize God's Word, it becomes a hiding place for you. And as we live each day in the fallen world, each one of us is going to need a hiding place in some way or another.

How has memorizing Scripture affected your outlook on life?

_____

The psalmist said, "I have chosen the way of truth; Your judgments I have laid before me" (Ps. 119:30).

Practically speaking, what does it look like to seek God with one's whole heart?

_____

We must make a choice to know God's Word. It doesn't come easy; it takes discipline. Yet if we want to keep ourselves pure, we must know the Word in our heads and stow the Word in our hearts.

Of course, there will be distractions, reasons why we should put off our Scripture reading. Plan for those times. Make an appointment with God each morning and don't break it—no matter what.

Remaining pure is a choice that we have to make. Daniel made that choice. It says that he purposed in his heart not to eat the king's meat. The psalmist made that choice. He wrote: "With my whole heart I have sought You; Oh, let me not wander from Your commandments" (Ps. 119:10).

We must choose to build upon the solid rock of God's Word. Nothing else is truly stable. If we base our lives on the ideas of our culture, we are like rock riddled with cracks, faults, and fractures. The rock crumbles under new pressures. It will not stand the test of time or the beating of the waves. The house built on that rock will fall, as if it were on sand. Yet if we build upon the Word of God, our house will stand forever. It rests on that solid faultless rock. Nothing the world has to offer as a foundation for our lives measures up to this precious, infallible, and inerrant Word.

If we know the Word and stow the Word in our hearts, then thirdly, the psalmist says we will keep the Word of God in our lives. We will show the Word by heeding the Word. And fourthly, he says we will keep it on our lips. We will sow the Word with our mouths.

Know the Word. Stow the Word. Show the Word. Sow the Word. Do these four things and you will quake-proof your life.

Respond personally to the questions in the margin on the left.

How much time do I spend each day in God's Word?

- ❏ Less than one TV show
- ❏ Less than a commercial
- ❏ None
- ❏ An adequate amount to quake-proof my life

• Do I spend more time absorbing the ways of this world than I spend in the Bible? ❏ Yes ❏ No

• Do I know the Word—do I aspire to study it from cover to cover? ❏ Yes ❏ No

• Do I regularly memorize God's Word? ❏ Yes ❏ No

• Am I quake-proofing my life by building it on the solid foundation of God's holy Word? ❏ Yes ❏ No

• Am I sharing God's Word with others so they too can quake-proof their lives and avoid disaster? ❏ Yes ❏ No

Before the Session

1. Prior to class, review Psalm 119. This psalm inspires us to live a life seeking the wisdom found in God's Word.
2. Consider collecting as many newspapers and other periodicals as possible from the past five days. Use these periodicals for the inter-active activity suggested below.
3. Bring tear sheets, colored markers, and tape (or a means to attach tear sheets to the wall).

During the Session

1. Place newspapers and other news-related periodicals on seats where learners typically sit. As learners arrive for class, ask them to pick up one of the periodicals and search it for examples of morality or the lack of morality. After people have had time to search through the news articles, ask: *What would you conclude about the state of morality in our community and in the world based on the articles you spotted?* Follow up by asking learners to share how they responded to the activity in Day 1.
2. Ask: *Looking at Days 2 and 3, what were the five "I's mentioned by Dr. Hawkins?* Next, as a class, read aloud Psalm 119:10-16. After reading, ask learners to share how they responded to the first interactive activity in Day 2. Explain that *relativism* was one of the main topics discussed in Day 2. Ask learners how they responded to the second interactive in Day 2. Ask: *Why is relativism often tied to a sense of intimidation toward those who believe in absolutes?*
3. Ask: *Why is isolation dangerous? How have you observed isolation affect your ability (or someone else's) to do what is right?* Remind learners that God created people to live in community with Him and with others. We think best when surrounding ourselves with people who can help us process our moral choices. In order to develop a list of healthy ways to fight isolation, ask learners to share their responses to the third interactive activity of Day 2.
4. Ask: *What did Dr. Hawkins mean when he said, "There exists a lot of imitation role models"?* Lead learners to see how Dr. Hawkins was

To the Leader:

In Dr. Hawkins's last lesson we are challenged to take measures to "quake proof" our lives. As you work through this lesson, make sure to review the whole series. Use the summary pages posted in your classroom to review with learners all the different themes that have been explored over the past weeks. In this lesson focus particularly on practical steps learners can take to live a life that is prepared for navigating the tough moral intersections that inevitably will come.

particularly referring to broken family systems that provide a poor imitation of healthy family systems. Ask learners to share how they responded to the first interactive in Day 3. [Be sensitive to information learners may share about their backgrounds and upbringings.]

5. Explain that a lot of information sources affect the way we think. Invite learners to share their responses to the second interactive for Day 3.

6. In wrapping up the discussion of Day 3's material, ask: *What did Dr. Hawkins mean by the word* inculcation? Use the final interactive for Day 3 to discuss the effect of inculcation.

7. Ask: *How does God's Word guard us against the five "I"s mentioned by Dr. Hawkins?* Use Psalm 119:18 to emphasize the importance of God's Word. Utilize both interactive activities for Day 4 to discuss how God's Word can help to protect us from moral fallout.

8. Ask learners to read Psalm 119:10-11,30,114. Ask: *How do these verses instruct us regarding God's Word?* Emphasize the importance of God's Word as our frontline defense against temptation. Explain that God's Word is a source of power and strength. Allow learners to share how they responded to the first interactive activity for Day 5.

9. Reread Psalm 119:10. Ask learners to share their responses to the second interactive exercise for Day 5. Emphasize that God's Word is a nonnegotiable part of our pursuit of our faith. We protect our lives as we build God's instruction into our lives. To challenge learners to consider how much they are investing in God's Word, ask them to share how they responded to the final interactive activity questions in the margin on page 166 (or give them time to respond).

10. Using a large sheet of paper, write on the top of the page the words *Quake-Proofing*. Under this title allow learners to list lessons learned from today's discussion and from Psalm 119. Then, using a different colored marker, ask learners to come up with one "take-away" application that this lesson teaches about how to protect one's self from a moral earthquake. Post the paper on the wall with the others.

11. Using the tear sheets, review all the lessons learned and the take-away emphases stressed during this series of lessons. Ask learners to discuss how these lessons will help them avoid secret fault lines and major earthquakes in their moral and Christian lives.